Dirty Pool: Playing to Win is a book for you if you want to beat your competition.

I heartily endorse Duane's new book. Duane brings both practical knowledge of billiards from years as a crack billiard mechanic as well as a sharp player's perspective to the table. *Dirty Pool: Playing to Win* is indeed a winner.
> **—Craig Connelly**
> **Founder and CEO, Connelly Billiards**

Dirty Pool: Playing to Win has two goals. One is to make you a better shooter; the other is to make you a better player. It does both admirably.
> **—Mike Janis**
> **President, The Viking Cue 9-ball Tour**

I definitely recommend *Dirty Pool: Playing to Win* to anyone wanting to learn more about playing pool to win.
> **—Shawn Putnam, Touring pro and three time Viking Tour overall champion**

Dirty Pool: Playing to Win, all chapters are organized in ten logical divisions intended to help you quickly understand what it takes to not only play pool, but how to win.

Dirty Pool: Playing to Win is a handy, concise, and informative book, chocked full of hints and pertinent illustrations on how to win at playing pool.

—Jack Baker, Indoor Outdoor Sports
Memphis Indiana

Dirty Pool: Playing to Win, like all of Duane's books, was written in an easy to read, straightforward language.

Dirty Pool: Playing to Win expertly explains how to—believe it or not—win.

Dirty Pool: Playing to Win is a book for anyone wanting to play pool and win.

Dirty Pool: Playing to Win details what all players want to know, how to win playing pool.

Dirty Pool: Playing to Win is more than a book on playing. It also covers some of the thoughts on how to win.

Dirty Pool: Playing to Win should be required reading for anyone wanting to learn how to win playing any cue sport.

—Keith Colby, Arizona Billiards

DIRTY POOL:
PLAYING TO WIN
FROM BEGINNING TO ADVANCED PLAYERS

Mose Duane

Phoenix Billiards
6133 W. Port-au-Prince Lane
Glendale, AZ 85306

Illustrated by the author
Cover by Erika A. Diehl
   www.erika.org
Cover photograph by On Location Photography
   Phoenix, Arizona
Printed by Print Partner
   Tempe, Arizona, United States of America

Publisher's Cataloging-in-Publication
(Provided by Quality Books, Inc.)

Duane, Mose.
   Dirty pool: playing to win: from beginning to
advanced players / Mose Duane. -- 1st ed.
   p. cm.
   Includes index.
   LCCN: 2002109750
   ISBN: 0967808952

   1. Pool (Games)   I. Title.

GV891.D83 2003   794.7'33
                         QBI02-200566

Other books by Mose Duane

The Billiard Guidebook:
A Complete, on the level, Manual of Maintenance,
Specifications, and Playing

Buying or Selling a Pool Table:
Ten Essential Components to
Consider Whether New or Used

Coming soon
Pool Table Maintenance and Repair:
From Basic to Professional

All books are available at bookstores,
on-line book sellers, pool table supply stores,
or directly from **PHOENIX BILLIARDS**
1-800-449-0804   1-602-843-0804
www.phoenixbilliards.com

ACKNOWLEDGMENTS

I would like to thank those whose encouragement and help was invaluable.

As always, Craig Connelly, Connelly Billiard Manufacturing, Inc., for the use of his tables, and personnel.

Of course, Steve Lunsford, Steve Lunsford Billiard Slates, for his belief in my endeavors from the beginning.

John and Nance Katrakis, Print Partner, whose advice and guidance were priceless.

Dave Carl, On Location Photography, for his fine work.

Keith Colby, who is still forced to read my stuff before anyone else.

Thomas Shaw, Pool & Billiard Magazine, for his continual kind words.

George Fels, Billiards Digest magazine, also for his kind words.

Steve Wester, for the gracious use of his saguaro.

Karen, my wife, for still putting up with me, after all these years.

And, of course, for all those who love this game.

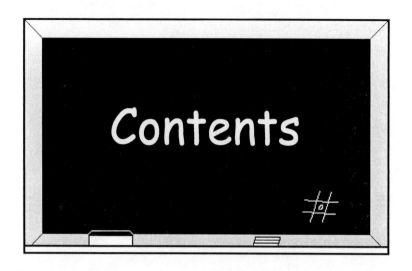

Contents

A pool hustler never hunts his mark.
Just like a mousetrap never hunts a mouse.

It's Only a Joke

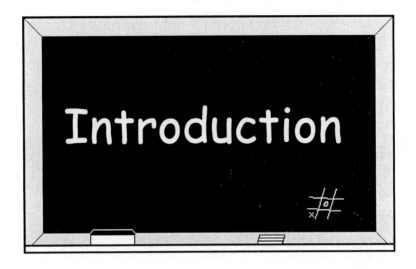

Introduction

I was introduced to the world of pool at the local Boy's Club in Columbus, Indiana at an impressionable age of ten or so. They had one nine-foot table that was always in desperate need of repairs because no one seemed willing or capable of doing the work. Imagine a ten-year-old even considering the lack of maintenance on anything, let alone a game he was just introduced to. But there I was, learning to play on a table with more ruts and valleys than a golf course. In spite of that, I learned enough about playing during those early years to later hustle the game when I was in the army at Fort Campbell Kentucky, and then in college at Indiana University.

In 1972, my then partner and lifelong friend, "Indy" Turner, and I opened a twenty-five-table poolroom we called *The Velvet Rail*. With the help of old timers like Art Schmidt of A. E. Schmidt Billiards, Paul Huebler of Huebler Cues, Gordon Hart of Viking Cues, BCA hall of fame inductee Minnesota Fats, and a local pool player named Fred Perry, Indy and I were quickly educated to the important phases of the billiard industry: playing, table maintenance, and of course hustling the game.

I stayed with pool, first in Indiana then twenty years in Arizona. I've made or refurbished hundreds of tables, moved, re-covered, and re-cushioned literally thousands of others in those years. And, of course, I've played pool. A lot. I've hustled and been hustled. Mostly, I played the cowboy way: in bars and "smoky old poolrooms."

Pool is a game of which I've made a profession. It has been good to me. Now that I have twenty plus (a big plus) years of pool table and playing knowledge, a pocketful of change (a small pocket), I feel obligated to give something back. *Dirty Pool: Playing to Win* is one of my offerings. It can cut, if not hours or days or months, then certainly years off the learning curve of playing to win.

To that end, then, this book has two goals. The first is to entice you into thinking in terms that will make you a better shooter by reviewing the fundamentals and the ten indispensable shots that

anyone remotely interested in winning must know
without hesitation or thought. Contending with the
fundamentals may at first sound trivial for anyone
except a beginning player, but it's crucial for all
players to reevaluate their basic game now and
again. Unused or overlooked skills deteriorate
quickly without review. To illustrate, answer this
question: If you off-aim an object ball to the left,
do you give the cue ball left english or right
english? Tick-tock, time's up. If you don't know or
had to stop and think about it, a review session is in
order. I've seen countless advanced players miss
shots because they wouldn't take the time to review
the fundamentals, or they tried silly, macho shots
when a simple shot or a safety would have been the
shrewd thing to do. To be a reliable shooter, you
must use common-sense shot making, be able to
control the cue and cue ball, have some idea where
the object ball will end up, and have the confidence
to do so shot after shot after shot after shot after
shot. That comes with practice and review.

The second goal is to present a different way of
thinking, or perhaps reinforce some of the thoughts
you already have, that will make you a better
player, and a more consistent winner. No, the two
goals aren't the same. You can be a great shooter,
but if you don't play to win, you won't. To
accomplish this goal, I give examples of
procedures you can use and rules you can abuse to

get you on track to thinking about winning. Would you ever, for instance, deliberately scratch; just aim the cue ball for a side pocket and let it rip? What if it might give you the advantage later in the game? Would you risk being called a dirty pool player for some minuscule advantage? I would. Every time I got the chance, especially if it meant winning instead of losing. And you should too, if you're serious about winning. The general rule is that if you scratch, your opponent gets the next shot with the cue ball in-hand. But the rule doesn't say you can't scratch. And it doesn't say you're going to get whopped upside the head if you do (maybe you will, depending on where you shoot, but that's not part of the rule). Anyway, as long as it gives you the advantage, it's worth the annoyance.

More times than I can remember, when I play a safety or a hook shot, I'd have players say: You're playing dirty pool, or, That's dirty pool. But to me, it's not dirty. To me, it's playing to win, and winning is what the game's all about whether I'm playing with the family or hustling beers, and that's the key.

Aren't you sick and tired of saying something like, oh well, it's only a friendly game, when you lose again and you know you're the better shooter. It may well be a friendly game, but someone has to win. It might as well be you, and it will be you, as long as you play every game to win.

Once you start thinking in terms of bending the rules to suit yourself, you'll look at the game in a completely different light, and I'm confident you'll come up with many other *dirty* ways to win on your own, because I haven't covered them all. Heck, I'm sure I don't know them all. But I guarantee you one thing: I'm always looking.

With a great deal of modifications in text and format, I have extrapolated portions of this book from my first book, ***The Billiard Guidebook***. And, like its predecessor, it is well illustrated with some of the same clear figures, and seeded with anecdotes, tips, and jokes I've picked up over the years.

Also, if you are not acquainted with frequently used pool or billiard terms, a short glossary has been placed at the end of the book. Take a few minutes to scan any unfamiliar terms. It will make your reading much easier.

And, finally, if you feel anything important has been left out of this book, or was not thoroughly and clearly expounded upon, please feel free to write. Usable suggestions will be rewarded with a free copy of the next revision.

Enjoy

Mose Duane

Two pool players were playing a long session
when one asked the other how he was able to get
out of the house so often and for so long.
"Even though my wife was never a pool player,
she is an angel," he answered. "What about you?"
"Well, the first player said," my wife's still alive,
so I have to sneak out of the house."

It's Only a Joke

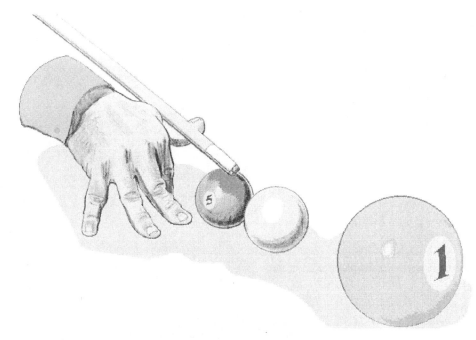

TEN WINNING
GAME FUNDAMENTALS

Building a solid game of pool is like building a
brick wall. The foundation must be laid first, then,
row by row, the structure assembled.

Learning to play winning pool, therefore, is the
foundation of your stance then, row by row;
balance, grip, bridge, stroke, english, and aim are
assembled, with shot making being the mortar that
holds them together. The break, lay of the table,
patterns, clusters, and shot selections are added for

strength, and, to top off the structure, include your mental and physical conditioning.

The fundamentals of the game should ultimately become second nature. The only way that will happen, though, is initially and periodically to think about what they are and how they relate to you. Thoroughly talk yourself through the following fundamentals during each practice session. But during the game, unless you're dogging your shots, let your subconscious deal with the fundamentals.

Winning Tip

The fundamentals of the game should ultimately become second nature.

Your fundamentals—or your favorite pro's fundamentals—may differ somewhat from those shown here, but if you're just learning, reviewing, or having trouble with some aspect of your game, follow these guidelines first; then, once your game picks up, you can mimic your favorite pro or make up your own fundamentals using whatever is comfortable or whatever works for you.

If, however, you think you already know the fundamentals or have your own down pat and purchased this book to find an easy way to win, then go ahead, skip this section and go directly to the winning practice shots or even on to the winning game elements and strategies. But if you really want to consistently win, you'll be back.

1. STANCE

The foundation of a winning pool game is stance, and, like any foundation, its most important feature is stability. Without stability, few good shots, if any, can be made consistently. On the other hand, because stance is not really a solid foundation, it must be tempered with comfort. If your stance is concrete solid, with every muscle straining for attention, not many good shots will be made either. You must strive for stability and comfort at the same time. And you can only achieve this by being relaxed and confident, confident not only in your ability, but also in your appearance as a pool player. You must look like a pool player; you must know you look like a pool player, and looking like a pool player starts with stance.

Winning Tip

You must look like a pool player, you must know you look like a pool player, and looking like a pool player starts with stance.

A few years ago, Mike, Jim, and "Strawberry" were regular customers at The Velvet Rail. They were good players and might have been excellent had it not been for stance. They could never achieve a proper stance because Jim and Strawberry were amputees and Mike was a double amputee.

I spent a lot of time with these guys and always felt blessed having known them. Despite their physical disabilities, they never gave up on the game they loved so much. (Jim was even an excellent ping-pong player.)

Whether hopping around the pool table on artificial limbs, one leg, crutches, or in a wheelchair, their stance was never taken for granted; they had to constantly adjust and readjust. Although they would moan, groan, and cuss like everyone else did when they missed a shot, they never blamed their disabilities.

These guys won their share of games, but of course, they could never be consistent winners because of their inability to develop a good stance. Most of us have the good fortune to have the use of both of our legs. Why not use them properly?

Unlike theirs, your stance, especially the distance from the table, will change depending on your shot. Some shots require that you be close to the table, often stretching across it; some shots require you to lean on the table; while other shots require you to step back and support your own weight. That was Mike, Jim, and Strawberry's downfall. They couldn't adjust that easily. But we can. Stance is the foundation of the rest of your game, don't take it for granted

In essence, the distance you stand from the table is determined by the position of the cue ball. To establish this distance, place your bridge hand behind the cue ball at the point where the bridge will be made (see section 4 of this chapter), then let your body find its own comfortable position from that point. Don't take up a stance at some arbitrary distance from the table, then try to stretch to the cue ball.

Although no two players will, or can, have the same stance, and each will eventually find his or her own best position, there are a few common factors all will share. Generally, to establish a sound stance, you should point your inside hip toward the table, and your outside hip between forty and fifty degrees away from the table. For stability, your feet should be positioned approximately shoulder width apart with your toes pointing slightly away from each other. Your outside foot should be set in front of your inside foot so that your outside foot's heel is approximately in line with your inside foot's arch (Figure 1-1).

Your inside knee and hip should be somewhat bent so that your body is comfortably leaning over the table.

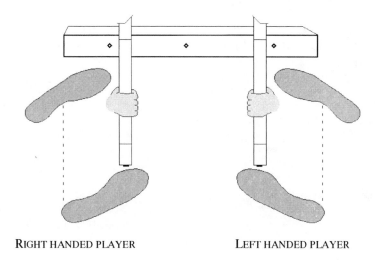

RIGHT HANDED PLAYER   LEFT HANDED PLAYER

Figure 1-1 *Stance*

Your outside forearm (the one stroking the cue), should be almost vertical from your elbow down so it can smoothly and freely swing in a pendular motion without interference from any other part of your body (Figure 1-2). Your head should be erect with your chin five to ten inches above the cue. Your eyes must aim along the cue shaft,

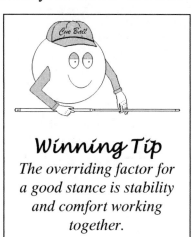

Winning Tip

The overriding factor for a good stance is stability and comfort working together.

and remain horizontal to take full advantage of your depth perception along the horizontal plane of the pool table. Never close one eye. A master rifleman uses both eyes; you should too.

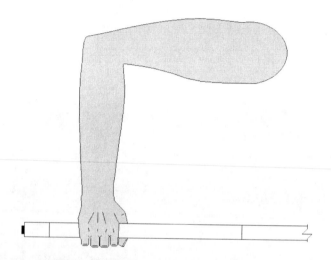

Figure 1-2 *Vertical arm*

The overriding factor for a good stance, then, is *stability* and *comfort* working together, with both eyes open and horizontal.

Your bridge hand is also part of your stance in that you lean some of your weight onto it, but that will be covered in more detail, in section 4 of this chapter.

2. CUES

The first row of bricks of the structure of winning pool is your cue and the way you use it.

Once you know how to win using the ten winning fundamentals of this book, although not ideal, you should be able to win using just about any cue, even one that is slightly warped. If you're ever forced to use a warped cue, make sure the warp or bow is hanging at the bottom of cue when you're stroking. This will prevent the cue form rolling or

Winning Tip

A good, straight, well-balanced cue will add ten to twenty percent to your game.

turning in your hand. However, having said that, a good, straight, well-balanced cue will add ten to twenty percent to your game. So, if you can run ten balls with any stick you pick up, you should be able to run eleven to twelve with a good cue. This is why I consider a good cue one of the ten winning fundamentals. And here is the sweet part: When you can consistently run ten to twelve balls, you can win any pool game, any time, against almost any player (excluding one or two of the pros, of course).

Cues generally weigh between 15 and 22 ounces. Although there's no right or wrong cue weight or size, as long as you're comfortable using the cue, most players use between 18 and 20 ounces.

ONE-PIECE CUES

High quality one-piece (house) cues are actually made from two pieces of wood. Maple is used for the shaft and rosewood, mahogany, maple, or some other hardwood for the butt. The two pieces are bonded together, normally using a four-prong splice but could have a flat face seam with the two halves pinned together (Figure 1-3).

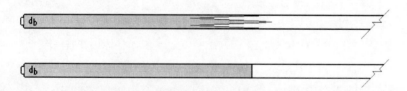

Figure 1-3 *One-piece cues*

The use of two pieces of wood is for more than decoration. Maple is used on the shaft for its hardness and trueness, while heavier woods are used for the butt to control the cue's weight distribution. Often, though, metal plugs or screws are inserted into the butt for added weight. High quality one-piece cues are excellent, inexpensive cues. They are well balanced, sized, and properly weighted. You should be able to play winning pool with any good quality one-piece cue. I've seen many excellent players simply pull a cue off the rack and go to work. Thinking you need a two hundred

Winning Tip

You should be able to play winning pool with any good quality one-piece cue.

dollar cue with five hundred dollars worth of junk inlays to play winning pool is a crutch; an excuse for not playing your best with what's available.

Don't get high quality, inexpensive one-piece cues confused with cheap department store cues made of soft, porous, or who knows what, woods that have no weight control or balance.

TWO-PIECE CUES

Two-piece cues are made from a variety of materials—fiberglass, aluminum, graphite, plastic sheathed wood, impregnated wood, layered wood, and on and on.

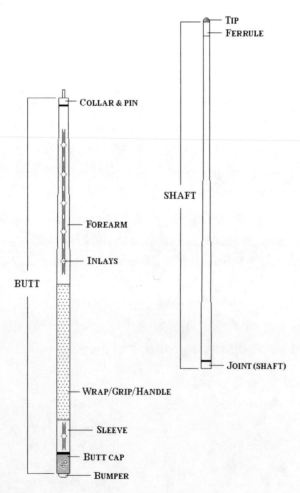

Figure 1-4 *Standard two-piece cue*

Non-wood and composite wood materials have come a long way in their ability to impart english on a cue ball, and the simple fact that they will not warp is a major advancement over wood. Still, the feel, consistent control, and beauty of wood cannot be duplicated.

The nomenclature used to describe a pool cue may differ somewhat depending on the area, manufacturer, and cost, but those depicted in Figure 1-4 are adequate to allow a thorough understanding of most cues.

Tips

Soft tips take chalk better than hard, but aren't as durable. Cuing the ball causes soft tips to compress and conform to the ball's shape, allowing for maximum contact. This makes soft tips more forgiving and less prone to miscuing.

Hard tips, on the other hand, will not give or contort much when they strike the cue ball. So, they must be chalked often, stroked with precision, and the cue ball must be hit closer to center to prevent miscuing. They will, however, add some speed to the cue ball.

Ferrules

Ferrules are sleeves or points installed on the end of the cue shaft to prevent the wood from splitting or splintering. Ferrules are made of plastic, fiber, Lucite, or phenolic. Plastic ferrules are used on cheap department store cues, and Lucite or phenolic on higher priced custom cues. Fiber ferrules are generally used on one-piece house cues, but can be found on some inexpensive custom cues.

The outside diameter of the ferrule will be the same as the cue shaft and tip, and the length can vary from ½ inch to a little over 1 inch. Ferrules are usually installed onto a tenon cut into the end of the shaft, or onto metal screws that are implanted into the shaft end (Figure 1-5).

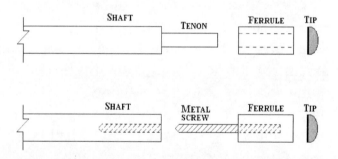

Figure 1-5 *Ferrules*

Shafts

Although other materials and other woods are used to manufacture cue shafts, maple is by far the most frequently used, and sugar maple is

considered excellent for cue shafts because of its
extremely dense, tight, and straight grain. Rock
maple, hard maple, and Canadian maple, are
different names given to the same sugar maple
wood.

Top quality shafts are always pro-tapered to
give them the same diameter from the cue tip back
ten to twelve inches toward the joint (Figure 1-6).
This helps you to create a solid, level stroke as the
cue slides through your bridge, and one of the
reasons a custom cue can add a few percentage
points to you game.

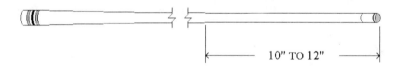

Figure 1-6 *Pro-taper*

The diameter of shafts at their tips, and along
their pro-tapers, range from 11 to 14 millimeters.
The ideal cue shaft size is said to be between 12
and 13 millimeters ($^{1}/_{2}$ inch), and, oddly enough,
$12^{1}/_{2}$ mm is what I prefer. The real size criterion,
though, is that a shaft should fit comfortably within
your closed bridge.

Joints

A two-piece cue shaft is mechanically attached to the butt by a joint. There are four basic kinds of cue joints: double screw, single screw, implex, and quick release.

1. A double screw joint is a double metal screw that turns into a double metal lug. Both halves of the joint are metal, usually stainless steel, so that the joining faces are metal to metal. The double screws, arranged one inside the other, makes an extremely stiff joint (joint 1 in Figure 1-7).

2. A single screw joint is a metal screw that turns into a metal lug. The two halves of the joint are metal and metal, plastic and metal, or plastic and plastic, with the metal screw in the center. This joint is stiff to medium stiff (joint 2 in Figure 1-7).

3. An implex joint is a metal screw that screws into a tapped hole in the end of the shaft, either directly into the wood or into a plastic or Lucite insert. The joining faces of an implex joint can be plastic to wood, but is usually wood to wood, making this joint the most flexible (joint 3 in Figure 1-7).

4. The quick release is a stainless steel or titanium pin that slips into a retaining insert in the shaft. Two or three quick turns lock the shaft into place. The joining faces are metal to plastic or fiber, or wood to wood, making this joint medium to flexible in stiffness (joint 4 in Figure 1-7).

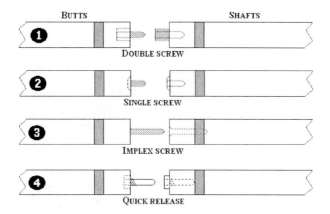

Figure 1-7 *Two-piece cue joints*

Which joint you choose to use is, of course, up to you and your game. Usually it makes little difference what you use, from a playability standpoint once you get used to a particular cue and joint, but generally a hard hitting player will use a solid metal to metal joint and a soft hitting, finesse player will want an implex, wood to wood joint.

Butts

Cue butts are also made of hardwood, or a combination of hardwoods, like ash, maple, and rosewood. Weight is controlled by using woods of different density, or metal plugs or screws inserted into the ends of the butts.

The diameter of a butt, in the griping area, ranges from $1^1/_2$ to 2 inches. Ultimately, though, butt size is determined by how comfortably it fits your hand.

To protect the end of the butt, it is fitted with a high impact plastic butt cap. A rubber bumper is inserted into the butt cap to save furniture and floors.

Depending on what you are willing to spend, the forearm and sleeve can be inlaid with an assortment of materials ranging from plastic to diamonds, including ebony, bone, mother-of-pearl, and dyed hardwoods.

However, inlays are usually not customized individually. Typically, custom cues are ordered by choosing the diameter of the shaft and butt, the weight of the cue, and the color or type of wrap.

The butt will be one of several pre-designed, pre-made, and mass-produced butts, with the inlays already embedded, and the most common of these inlays is mother-of-pearl and colorful hardwoods.

The entire cue butt can be left with exposed wood, but for better grasping, the griping area is usually wrapped in nylon, leather, or Irish linen. Ignoring preference and feel, the only advantage of one wrap over the other is either aesthetic or cost, with nylon being the cheapest (sometimes even cheaper than finished wood), and linen being the most expensive and having the greatest visual appeal.

CUE CARE

Unless specifically purchased without, most cues come with a urethane or varnish finish. You should remove this finish from the shaft with extra-fine 600-grit sandpaper or 0000-grit steel wool.

Lightly sand about 10 inches from the ferrule toward the joint—the distance of a pro-taper. The cue should never be sanded again. Period. Ever. Some players have a habit of sanding the shaft occasionally to keep it slick and smooth. Over time, this makes the shaft smaller in diameter. A better method is to use a cloth

Winning Tip
Powder and talc are self-defeating, the more they are used the dirtier the cue shaft becomes. The dirtier the shaft is, the more it will need to be powdered.

dampened with a solution of cool water and mild soap. Wipe the mixture on and off quickly. Don't soak it. From then on, as sweat and dirt builds up, use a small synthetic household scrub pad like

Scotch Bright (but not steel wool) to keep the shaft clean and slick. You need nothing else, not even powder or talc. Actually, powder and talc are self-defeating, the more they are used the dirtier the shaft becomes. The dirtier the shaft is, the more it will need to be powdered. It is simply not necessary when a damp cloth and scrub pad will do the job better. Also, a few products on the market are designed to make a cue slick without powders, sandpaper, or mess, and are worth trying.

A cue should never be leaned against the pool table or wall, even between shots. If possible, try to stand the cue straight up in a cue rack. If it must be supported by the table or wall, keep it as perpendicular as possible, with no side load on the shaft. Laying a cue flat on the pool table playing surface is okay for short periods, but avoid storing it like that. When a cue is lying flat, the tip end of the shaft may not be supported, and gravity will eventually take its toll.

Always store one-piece cues in a cue rack, either floor or wall mounted. Break down two-piece cues and store them in a cue case, preferably one that is hard and sturdy. Don't store any cue in places of extreme temperature and humidity variances, such as cars, attics, damp basements, etc.

The cue tip should be rough to hold chalk, and crowned so a rounded surface will be striking the ball. However, a shoulder should be left between the beginning of the crown and the tip's base at the top of the ferrule. A good rule-of-thumb is that the crown of the tip should have the same arc as the circumference of a U.S. penny (Figure 1-8).

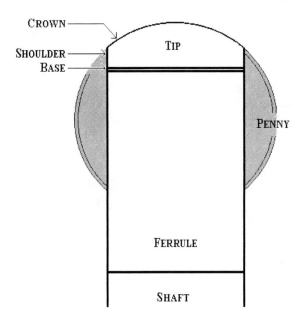

Figure 1-8 *Cue tip*

Instead of a penny, some players use a nickel, while others prefer a dime. The arc of a penny falls between those two, and has an almost ideal circumference. Several cue tip shaping tools now on the market make the job a snap, but the crown can be shaped with a file or 60-grit sandpaper, if care is taken. Always sand down toward the ferrule; that is, don't pull the tip up and away from its bond.

Cue tips compress and flatten during play, and should be shaped periodically, not just when they are replaced.

Winning Tip

In the end, you don't need to have an expensive cue to win. Almost any low end, name brand cue will do just fine.

In the end, you don't need to have an expensive cue to win. In fact, an overly expensive cue could have a negative effect on your game by putting pressure on you to try to perform up to its cost. Almost any low end, brand name cue will do just fine, as long as it is balanced, clean, and has a pro-taper. I like "Sneaky Pete cues," "Hustlers cues," "Two-piece House cues," or whatever you want to call them, over any showy or gaudy cue.

3. BALANCE AND GRIP

I've seen players grip the cue forward of the grip and I've seen some grip it back at the butt, and still play decent pool. But, in the long run, they don't win, because the cue isn't balanced, and in both cases, they have to grip it far too tight and are constantly straining for control. You'll eventually find a balance and gripping style that suites you, even if it is slightly different from what follows, but what follows is fundamentally sound.

To find the best balance point, slide your grip hand along the butt until the cue's weight equalizes, then move your hand an inch or two backward to make the balance slightly shaft heavy. This grip position, along with being more comfortable than a true balance, will help keep the cue from jumping up during a stroke, especially when you're using an open bridge.

Cradle the butt between your thumb and fingers, but slightly below your palm (Figure 1-9). Be firm in your grip. The cue must not slip when it strikes the ball, and power must be supplied by a firm grip. However, although a firm grip is necessary, don't choke the cue. Excessive gripping will cause poking and jabbing, undue strain on your gripping hand and arm—and sweaty palms and white

knuckles. You'll look like you're scared to death,
instead of relaxed, and like you came to lose,
instead of win.

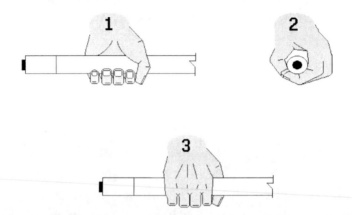

Figure 1-9 *Correct grip*

Also, hold the cue level, or as near level as

Winning Tip

*Grip the cue firmly, but
don't choke it, and hold it
level or as near level as
possible with every shot.*

possible with every shot.
Change english by also
changing the elevation of
your bridge, not just the
butt of the cue. This, as
much as anything else
you can do, will help
prevent unwanted
english or spin on the
cue ball, and give you far
better control.

4. BRIDGE

HAND BRIDGE

Your bridge has to be as firm and as stable as any row of bricks in any wall, and is as important as your stance; indeed, it is an integral part of your stance. Your bridge arm can be straight or slightly bent, but it must support some of your upper body weight, and, therefore, become part of your stance because you will be leaning onto it. If your arm, hand, and bridge are weak, your shot will also be weak.

Place your bridge hand behind the cue ball at the point where the bridge will be made, then let your body find its own comfortable position from that point. For most players, the distance from the bridge to the cue ball is about eight inches, although some players shorten it for near shots to four to six inches and lengthen it for long shots to ten inches or more. But eight inches is the ideal distance for a starting position, and it works fine for both near and long shots. I try to never change mine. It's just an added complication I don't need.

An easy bridge to make is the open bridge. This is accomplished by placing your bridge hand flat on the table with your fingers spread apart (hand 1 in Figure 1-10).

Then, keeping your fingers stiff and on the table, pull your fingertips in. This will force the palm of your hand an inch or so off the table. Next, place your thumb high on your index finger to form a V between that thumb and the knuckle of your index finger (hand 2 in Figure 1-10). This V forms the open bridge (hand 3 in Figure 1-10).

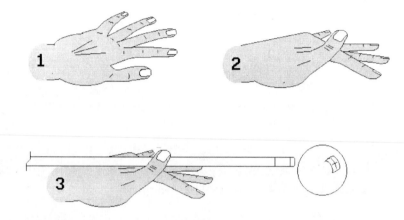

Figure 1-10 *Open bridge*

The open bridge is a good bridge for beginners and those who cannot, for one reason or another, physically fold their hand to form a closed bridge. The problem with an open bridge, though, is that it allows the cue to jump up when the cue ball is struck, particularly when using high english.

A version of the open bridge is also used when you must shoot over a ball. This bridge is made as if it were an open bridge except the heel of your hand is raised from the table, and your index and little fingers are moved beneath your hand to help support it. This elevates the bridge above the obstructing ball (bridge 1 in Figure 1-11).

Cue balls that are less than a bridge distance from the rail can be cued using the rail and your bridge hand's fingers as a bridge. With the cue lying on the rail, place your bridge hand over it, allowing the cue to slide between your index finger and middle finger. Use your thumb and little finger for support on the top or outside edge of the rail (bridge 2 in Figure 1-11). On a wide rail, however, tucking your thumb beneath your palm for added support, though awkward and uncomfortable, is often necessary.

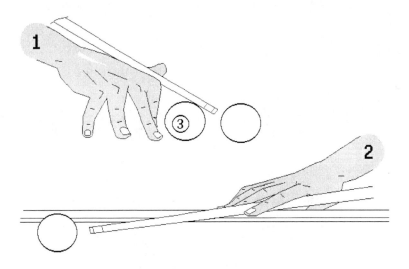

Figure 1-11 *Elevated and rail bridges*

The preferred bridge, however, is the closed or loop bridge. This bridge is accomplished by making a circle with your thumb and index finger, as if making an "okay" sign. Place the circle on the table, and, simultaneously, force your other three fingers apart (hand 1 in Figure 1-12).

Winning Tip

Remember: Your bridge arm and hand are part of your stance, and must support some weight.

Keeping your fingertips on the table, pull your middle finger beneath the circle at your thumb and index finger, which, along with your palm, will lift from the table. Support the bridge by three fingers (little, ring, and middle), and the heel of your hand (hand 2 in Figure 1-12).

The cue will slide within the circle of your thumb and index finger, and on top of your middle finger (hand 3 in Figure 1-12). Tighten your hold on the cue shaft by flexing the first joint of your index finger, the tighter the better (hand 4 in Figure 1-12).

As with all bridges it is important to keep your bridge hand and arm solid by keeping some weight on them. Remember: your bridge arm and hand are part of your stance.

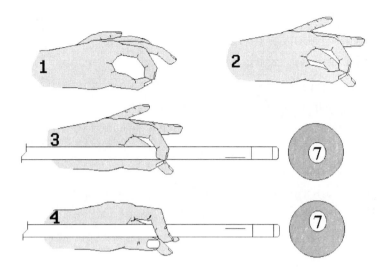

Figure 1-12 *Preferred bridge*

Fred Perry was a local pool player who came into the Velvet Rail almost daily. If he wasn't playing some hustler from out of town, he was either trying to hustle me in One Pocket or ping-pong, or he was practicing pool shots. His favorite games were Nine Ball, One Pocket, and Bank.

Fred taught me more about making a bridge than I would have thought possible. He had the smoothest stroke, and firmest, best looking bridge I had ever seen. As weird as it sounds, he could clamp the cue shaft between his middle finger, ring finger, and thumb and make it look like the most natural thing in the world.

Most of us can't do what he did because we have an index finger in the way. He took care of that problem some time before I met him. Fred was a house painter, and one day after his sprayer clogged, he stuck his index finger over the orifice of the spray head and pulled the trigger to build up enough pressure to unclog it. At that second, the clog dislodged itself, and the sprayer blew paint up the end of his finger. "The miserable thing," he told me, "ballooned like a hotdog on a stick, and exploded as I watched."

The doctors wanted to amputate what was left of his finger at the second joint, leaving a one-joint stub. But Fred had the foresight to insist that they take it off all the way back at the knuckle so the stub wouldn't interfere with his bridge.

As the wound healed, Fred practiced using his middle finger to take the place of his index finger and his ring finger to take the place of his middle finger. Within a year, his bridge looked as natural as any. I'd known him for several months before I realized that his "oh so natural" bridge was literally the result of months of dogged determination on his part.

I always figured that if he could make a respectable bridge using his middle finger, then anyone should be able to make one using his or her index finger. It may take a lot of finger contorting effort, but, as cumbersome as it first feels, a stable bridge can be made.

Although making a bridge is fundamental, it is extremely important, if you came to win. You must be able to make a solid, tight bridge, and be just as dedicated at it as Fred was.

MECHANICAL BRIDGE

How can a "sissy stick," "granny stick," or "crutch," be a fundamental of the game? The most important way I can think of is that you can't be a consistent winner without it. Mechanical bridges are designed to allow you to extend across the table for shots you couldn't reach otherwise, and they also provide you with a means to play over a ball that has blocked the cue ball. If you try to make these shots by any other method, you risk missing the shot and losing the game, and you're here to win. Right? I've seen players play ambidextrous or behind their backs or one handed to avoid using a

Winning Tip

If the bridge is not solid, whether it's mechanical or hand, you might just as well close your eyes and poke at the ball.

mechanical bridge. How absurd! They even practice these shots! How bizarre is that?

When using a mechanical bridge, place the bridge head six to eight inches from the cue ball, rest the bridge stick (handle, grip, or whatever you want to call it) on the playing surface and firmly press it down to insure that it's solid and that some of your weight is distributed onto it. Don't hold the bridge stick like it's another cue, or wave it around like a flagpole. If the bridge is not solid, whether it's mechanical or hand, you might just as well close your eyes and poke at the ball. And you certainly can't win with your eyes shut! At least, I can't.

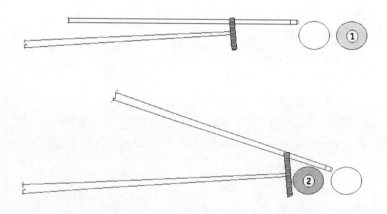

Figure 1-13 *Mechanical bridge*

If you have to cue over an object ball, turn the bridge head on its side to make it taller, but still rest the butt on the table for stability. Hold the cue by its end and aim down its length (2-ball bridge in Figure 1-13).

Most professionals say to hold the cue up and aim down its length anytime you use a mechanical bridge, just like shooting over an object ball. Okay, that's valid on most shots. But on shots where nothing is in your way, I like to hold the cue as level as

Winning Tip

A mechanical bridge is just as much a part of the game as is any other accessory. Use it.

possible, play slight follow english—nothing fancy—like it's any other shot (1-ball bridge in Figure 1-13).

The mechanical bridge is just as much a part of the game as is any other accessory. Use it. Let your opponents snicker if they want, but remember, it's their beer you're drinking.

5. STROKE

Another row of bricks in your structure is a smooth winning stroke, and, even though it's not particularly difficult, it's astonishing to me how otherwise excellent players abuse it. Stroking is the rhythmic back and forth gliding of the cue across or

Winning Tip

You must think about what you want to happen. If you brain doesn't know what it wants, how is your body and arm going to know?

through your bridge before the cue ball is impacted, and then carrying through to follow the cue ball after impact. Without this series of motions, the tendency is to poke or jab at the cue ball causing it to lurch forward, or worse, to deflect to one side or the other instead of tracking your intended path.

Stroking allows your body, eyes, and the cue to be aligned for the shot, and for your body and arm to get the feel of what your brain wants them to do. Still, in order for this to work you must *think* about what you want to happen. If your brain doesn't know what it wants, how is your body and arm going to know?

And this is the time to concentrate. If you want low, right english, make sure the cue tip is going to hit the low, right quadrant of the cue ball. Be smooth. Think. Concentrate. Bam! Good shot. Easy stuff.

6. CUING THE BALL

Cuing the ball properly is also as important as any row of bricks in any wall, but few novice, and even some advanced players really understand what it does other than move the cue ball. Cuing the ball is an extension of the series of stroking motions; the constant forward action of your final stroke.

Add a little speed for power but don't allow the cue tip to slide off the cue ball—that's what a tight bridge is all about. You can actually force the cue to remain on a straight path by keeping a tight bridge and following through. This means keeping the cue following the shot as if you're trying to force it through the cue ball. It also means keeping the cue level; the butt must follow the tip. This is following through, and it's just as important in pool as it is in any other game or sport.

Following through determines the path of the cue ball as much as anything else. This is even true with a stop or draw shot, where many players, novice and above, try to jab at the cue ball for fear they cannot get the cue out of

Winning Tip
Following through is not some separate entity. It is an integral part of your stroke.

the way of the cue ball's recoil. Follow through is not some separate entity. It is an integral part of your stroke.

Prior to cuing the ball, your stroke must be smooth and graceful. If it's erratic, if the butt of the cue swings left, right, up, or down, even slightly, during the cuing stroke it will impart spin on the cue ball and you'll never know it. You'll miss a shot that is perfectly aimed and have no idea why. Again, the cue must be held as near level as possible, and stroked on a plane in which the butt follows the tip (Figure 1-14).

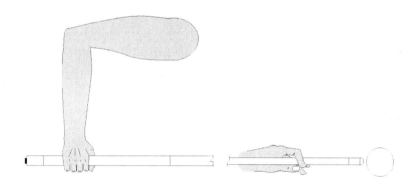

Figure 1-14 *Level stroke*

Any stroke off dead center of the cue ball imparts some kind of spin, wanted or not. Far too many players do it unintentionally by not concentrating, by not being smooth, by using a sloppy bridge, etc.

Winning Tip

Any stroke off dead center of the cue ball imparts some kind of spin, wanted or not.

Even worse, some "hotshots" cue the ball off center needlessly because they think it's the only way to make a shot, or that the spinning cue ball looks "cool." They fail to understand or believe that most shots can be made without any spin at all.

Unwanted or unneeded spin is particularly crucial if there's considerable distance between the cue ball and the object ball. Shooting a cue ball the length of a standard table with one cue tip diameter off to the right will cause the cue ball to deflect right as much as a ball's width, or more depending on how hard the ball is hit and the condition of the cloth. Avoiding long side spinning shots at any level of play is advisable, especially if you're playing to win.

So, to impart controlled and planned spin on the cue ball, it must be struck firmly with precision and forethought. These are accomplished with a smooth *stroke* and *follow through*. Jabbing or poking will only cause the cue ball to slide away from its intended path.

Winning Tip

To impart controlled and planned spin on the cue ball, it must be struck firmly with precision and forethought.

7. ENGLISH

English has two purposes. One is to intentionally change the direction of the object ball, hopefully to make the shot easier, and the other is to change the direction of the cue ball, especially after it strikes the object ball, so it can be positioned for the next shot. Unfortunately, these two individual results of english occur at the same time. Playing one will also get the other, so allowances must be made.

English on the cue ball will result in opposite english on the object ball for a short distance. If you want the object ball to spin left, then right english must be applied on the cue ball, and so on. This is useful in that it "opens" the pocket, in effect making a larger target. That is, if you are aware that left english causes the object ball to move right, you can off-aim to the left of the pocket and still make the shot.

Winning Tip

Left english causes the object ball to move right, you can off-aim to the left of the pocket and still make the shot.

However, cue ball position is the most significant purpose of english. This is the process of putting the cue ball in some position so the next object ball will be set up for a plausible shot.

Seasoned players will carry this forward to the point of thinking three or four shots in advance, making each shot and leaving the cue ball in position for the next. They will be able to position the cue ball within a few inches of their next shot, and lined up for a good play at the next ball. Imagine how easy the game is when you can position the cue ball so that every shot becomes an easy, almost straight in shot. That's what playing to win is all about, making every shot easy, instead of playing one difficult shot after another.

Beginners should, at first anyway, try to get the cue ball to the same end of the table as their next shot, then the same end and same side. As they gain experience, they can narrow the range until the cue ball is stopping in the general area of the next object ball; an area that could be called the Cone of Position, and this is usually good enough (see *Cue Ball Position* in the next section).

Essentially, then, english is the controlled spin put on the cue ball by the cue. So, in varying degrees across the axis of the ball, there are five kinds of english: follow, stop (center or no english), draw, left, and right (Figure 1-15).

Follow english is accomplished by cuing the cue ball along the top of its vertical axis (ball 1, and line segment SF of ball 6 in Figure 1-15). This forces the cue ball to spin forward and *follow* the object ball after striking it. (Technically the object ball should spin backward, but because of cloth friction it rolls forward from the point of contact.)

A stop shot is accomplished by cuing the cue ball dead center (ball 2 in Figure 1-15). Because the cue ball is primarily sliding, it will *stop* after it strikes the object ball. The object ball will roll straight forward from the point of contact.

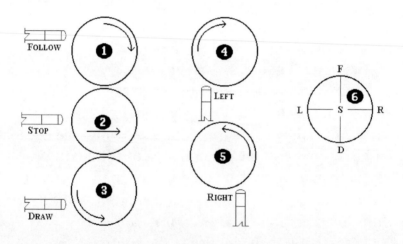

Figure 1-15 *Basic english*

Draw english is accomplished by cuing the cue ball along the bottom of its vertical axis (ball 3, and line segment SD of ball 6 in Figure 1-15). This forces the cue ball to spin backward and *draw* away from the object ball after it makes contact. The object ball will roll forward from the point of contact. A small (around 5° and certainly less than 10°) butt high angle will force more friction between the cue ball and the cloth to give you a slightly quicker draw, but, because I don't care for massé shots of any kind, this is the only time I would recommend a butt high stroke.

Left english is accomplished by cuing the cue ball along the left horizontal axis (ball 4, and line segment SL of ball 6 in Figure 1-15). This causes the cue ball to spin *left* and, to a lesser degree, the object ball to spin right as it moves from the point of contact.

Right english is accomplished by cuing the cue ball along the right side of its horizontal axis (ball 5, and line segment SR of ball 6 in Figure 1-15). This causes the cue ball to spin to the *right* and, to a lesser degree, the object ball to spin left as it moves from the point of contact.

There are innumerable points of contact along a cue ball's vertical and horizontal axis in which

Winning Tip

There are only nine feasible english shots that you'll need to win at any pool game: stop (center), follow, draw, right, left, follow right, follow left, draw right, and draw left.

to impart english. As the cue tip moves out from the center of the cue ball, more english is automatically added—from zero at dead center to something near uncontrollable english at the outer edge. To complicate matters, combinations of english can be given to a cue ball by striking it somewhere in either quadrant of the vertical and horizontal axis. Any strike in quadrant FSR of ball six in Figure 1-15, for example, imparts follow and right english simultaneously. Looking at it from that perspective, the variations of english are endless.

Fortunately, though, for winning players, english variations can be narrowed down immensely. The cue should never strike the cue ball more than one cue tip diameter distance from the center of the ball because anything greater causes miscues without generating a significantly more *controllable* spin to the cue ball, and anything less is generally too subtle to be effective.

This means that there are only nine feasible english shots (or cuing points) that you'll need to win at any pool game (Figure 1-16). These nine shots are stop (center), follow, draw, right, left, follow right, follow left, draw right, and draw left. Unless you are a professional player, anything else is a joke and should be left to show-offs and trick shot artists. If you start making high-spin, low percentage shots consistently, you'll find yourself

either on the cover of Billiards Digest or Pool &
Billiard Magazine, or on the corner table playing
with (by) yourself, which is more likely. Know
what I mean?

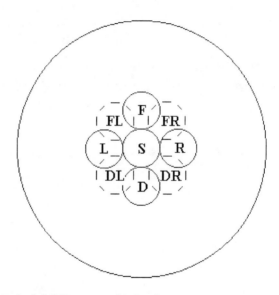

Figure 1-16 *Nine english shots*

8. EFFECTS OF ENGLISH

NON-CUSHION SHOTS

It's interesting how much control you can gain over the cue ball by using only the nine english shots depicted in Figure 1-16. This is easy to see by imagining a circle of some arbitrary diameter on the playing surface, adjacent to a center pocket with the center of the circle half a ball's diameter behind some object ball, and the cue ball on the circle's circumference, but with both balls aligned with the pocket (Figure 1-17).

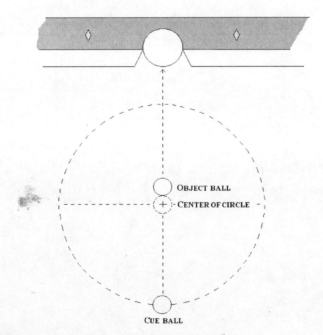

Figure 1-17 *Align balls with pocket*

What would happen if you cued the cue ball using no side english? Stop would send the object ball into the pocket and the cue ball would stop in the center of the circle, at approximately half a ball's diameter behind where the object ball was, S in Figure 1-18. Draw would bring the cue ball back to D, and the cue ball would stop at F with follow.

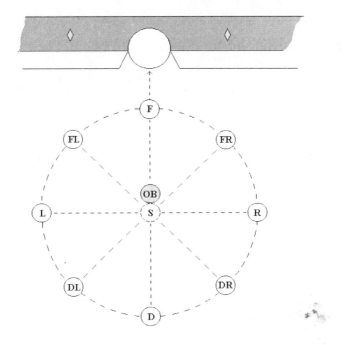

Figure 1-18 *Nine cue ball positions*

Now, imagine what would happen if you use the six side english shots. Theoretically, assuming you can generate the same power with each shot, the cue ball will stop at the intersection of the circle's circumference and the radial of the english shot used. That is, if you use right english, the cue ball will stop at R in Figure 1-18, and if you use draw left english, the cue ball will stop at DL, and so forth.

That's the theory anyway.

Throw

In reality, you're not going to achieve a perfect circle, and if you can get anywhere in close proximity to R and L using right and left english alone, you're doing fine because it's a tough shot.

The reason is twofold. One, it's rare to find an average player (or even an above average player) who can cue the cue ball perfectly every time. At times even pro players have their problems. Often some small amount of draw or follow english will be applied along with left or right. But that's part of the challenge of the game! Right?

The second reason is stroke. If the cue isn't stroked precisely, the cue ball will take a slightly different path than intended, and will not strike the object ball dead on, sending the cue ball slightly askew. Everything will work out, of course, because when you make the shot the cue ball will end up in the vicinity of L or R, if not exactly on the circle's circumference.

Also, if you tried to shoot the object ball straight into the pocket using, say, DL english, you could miss the shot to the right. This happens because when using english the path of the object ball will be displaced in the opposite direction of the english. This deflection is usually referred to as throw.

Throw can be used to deflect a ball to a pocket that it isn't lined up with (1 ball in figure 1-19), instead of cutting it in (2 ball in figure 1-19). Either way, you make the ball in the same pocket, using the same english. But, the important thing here is that you end up with two different positions of the cue ball.

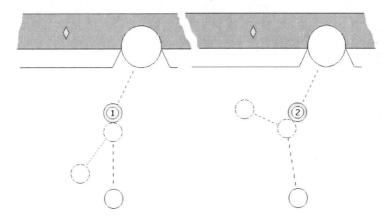

Figure 1-19 *Throw shot vs. cut shot*

Or, throw can be used to make an object ball that is lined up with the pocket, but because you

want the cue ball to end up at a particular position,
you can't cut or shoot the object ball straight in.

So, in order to insure making all the shots in the
cue ball position circle and leaving the cue ball on
the circle's circumference, you must off-aim the
object ball a little and throw it into the pocket.
Remember that the object ball will deflect slightly
in the opposite direction of the english, so you must
off-aim on the side of the english: left english, off-
aim left to throw the ball right, etc. (Figure 1-20).

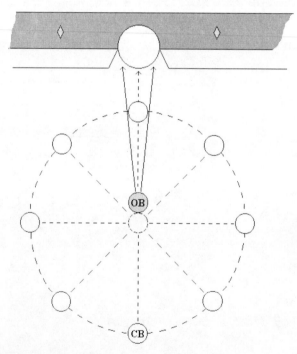

Figure 1-20 *Off aim for position*

The amount of off aiming is a matter of how hard the ball is struck and how far it must travel. Usually aiming for the edge of the pocket (or second object ball for carom shots) instead of the center is adequate.

Further, because the diameter of the circle is controlled by the power of your stroke, it can be increased by increasing power, and decreased by decreasing power. This would also increase and decrease the throw.

Winning Tip

Off aim on the side of the english: left english, off aim left, right english, off aim right.

Understanding this concept will add to your performance immeasurably, and help you develop a more consistent finesse stroke. And that'll put you on the track to winning.

Cue Ball Position

Although cue ball position may be the most significant purpose of english, I don't want to imply that english is the only way to get position. Natural positioning, simply letting the cue ball roll to the next shot without side english, is a plausible (and sometimes preferable) means of getting position. Just make the shot and let both balls roll, and control your position by power. It's that simple.

But usually some english is applied, and if the cue ball hits the object ball before that english takes affect the object ball will react as if no side english had been used. This is typically referred to as neutral english.

Neutral english has been called other things like, natural english, sliding english, stun english (when struck hard), and probably lots more that I'm not aware of. But it simply means that, although english is applied, the cue ball is still sliding when it makes contact with the object ball. When a sliding cue ball impacts an object ball, not only will the object ball react as if there's no english, the cue ball will leave the point of contact at a ninety degree tangent . . . every time, no matter what speed it's traveling or how much english is applied. But if the english takes before the cue ball makes contact with the object ball, the cue ball will leave the contact point in a slightly different direction. This is important when considering position play because all other degrees or lines from the object ball can be judged from the ninety-degree tangent line.

Winning Tip

Natural positioning is simply letting the cue ball roll to the next shot, using neutral english.

Consider Figure 1-21, when high english takes affect before contact with an object ball that's struck other than straight on, the angle (in relation to the tangent line) in which the cue ball travels will increase, when low english takes, the angle will decrease.

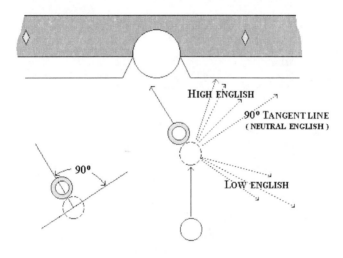

Figure 1-21 *Tangent line*

The amount of increase and decrease depends on how much english you apply, how hard you stroke the cue ball, and the distance the cue ball is from the object ball.

And, of course, whether the cue ball is still sliding on contact also depends on how far apart the two balls are and how hard you shoot. The trick is to figure out how hard *you* must stroke the cue for any given shot, and this only comes with practice. But now, at least, you have some means of judging.

Cone of Position

Again, that's the theory. That's what happens in a perfect world, on a perfect table, with a perfect stroke (and if you're good looking, otherwise you don't stand a chance anyway!). But, even though all is not ideal in the world of pool tables, you can win without perfection. In fact, it's often not even advisable to try for perfect position on every shot, especially for anyone below an intermediate level. Just getting the cue ball in the neighborhood of the next ball is usually good enough—as long as it's the right neighborhood. This is a valid idea for a couple of reasons. One, the object ball can still be made a few inches on either side of the "perfect" position, and, two, by trying to achieve the perfect position, you risk missing the present shot—the one that really matters. The best position in the world does you no good if you relinquish your turn at the table.

Visualize where the cue ball would have to be in order for the next shot to be perfect, straight in, or at least easy. Now imagine a cone funneling back from the object ball at some realistic width that would allow you to make the object ball from anywhere within the cone, *and still get shape on the next ball.* In Figure 1-22, you can make the 7 ball, end up anywhere in cone A, make the 8 ball, and still get shape (anywhere in cone B) to make the 9 ball.

The important thing to remember when you're making an english position shot is that the object ball must be off aimed a little in the direction of the cue ball english because it will travel in the opposite direction. Once more, if right english is needed, for example, you should aim the object ball slightly to the right of the intended target to "throw" it left and into the target.

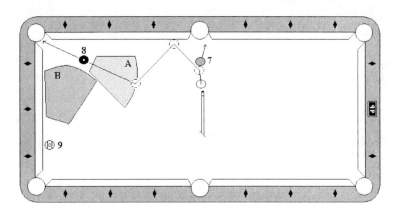

Figure 1-22 *Cone of Position*

CUSHION SHOTS

Since cushions make up a significant amount of any pool game, it's imperative that you understand what's going to happen when a ball rebounds from one or more cushions. It's amazing how may good players I run into that still don't quite grasp this concept, and you can't win consistently without this understanding. But, if it's taken one step at a time, it isn't really as complicated as Figure 1-23 might indicate.

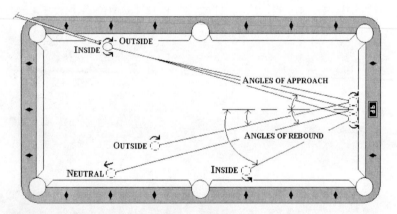

Figure 1-23 *Effects of english*

No Side English

A ball with no side english will rebound from a rail at the same angle it approaches the rail. A ball approaching at, say, 30°, will rebound at 30° in the opposite direction. If it approaches straight on (0°)

it will rebound straight back, and so on. That's basic geometry and intuitive to understand, but the interesting thing to note is what happens when side english is applied.

Ball Deflection

When the cue ball is cued the length of the table it can curve (ball deflection) as much as one ball's width in the direction of the english, if it's struck hard enough. This is depicted in Figure 1-23 in the different points at which the cue ball contacts the head rail. If the ball didn't deflect, it would contact the rail at the same spot no matter what english you used.

However, as the cuing distance is

Winning Tip

Since you're thinking in terms of winning games, most shots should be short, less than a quarter of a table's width.

shortened the deflection will be less, down to almost nothing at about one quarter of the table's width. This happens because a firmly hit ball will slide for some distance, or there will be less table roll because of the smaller space, or both. But, past that point, once english takes, there's no real way to determine precisely where the ball will hit, except on a perfect table under perfect conditions, maybe. So, generally, it's a guess or estimation of sorts, though, the more you practice, the more precise your estimation will be. But, in the end, as precise as you may be, it's still a guess. Therefore, since you're now thinking in terms of winning games, most shots should be kept short, less than a quarter of a table's width if you can manage it, and all long shots should be ignored or performed without english during a game, or regulated to the "only if nothing else is available" category of shots.

Inside / Outside english

When talking about english and angles, two terms are used to eliminate confusion over left and right english. Spin applied to the inside of the angle

Winning Tip

Inside english increases or opens the angle of rebound, and outside english decreased or closes the angle of rebound.

of approach is called *inside* english and spin applied to the outside is *outside* english.

In Figure 1-24, right english is inside and left english is outside. When that same shot is performed from the other side of the table, left english is inside and right english is outside.

Basically, inside english increases or opens the angle of rebound, and outside english decreases or closes the angle of rebound. This holds true if the ball rebounds from adjacent cushions. That is, inside english will continue to increase the angle, and outside english will continue to decrease the angle as the ball rebounds around the table until friction stops it from spinning (Figure 1-24).

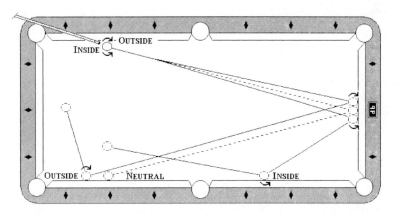

Figure 1-24 *Rebounds from adjacent cushions*

The amount of opening or closing depends on how much english is applied, how hard the ball is struck (slower balls succumb more quickly to friction), and the condition of the bed cloth.

But what happens when the ball rebounds from opposing rails? Nope, it's not the same thing (duh!). It's actually the opposite. When a ball rebounds from an opposite cushion, side english will reverse on each rebound after the first (Figure 1-25).

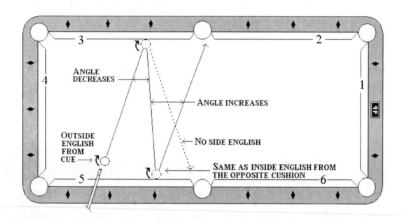

Figure 1-25 *Cue ball reverses english*

Except to be less severe each time it rebounds because of friction, the spin on the ball does not change. What changes is the ball's spin *in relation* to the rail it's approaching.

Figure 1-25 shows outside english being cued from the vicinity of rail five, which decreases the angle of rebound from rail three. When the ball reaches rail five again, however, it is spinning as if it were cued from rail three with inside english, which increases the angle of the second rebound at rail five.

Further, as if that's not enough, because the object ball spins in the opposite direction as the cue ball when english is applied, everything reverses again when the object ball comes into play.

To make the same shot depicted in Figure 1-25 when using an object ball instead of just a cue ball, you would have to cue opposite english, or, in this example, inside instead of outside (Figure 1-26).

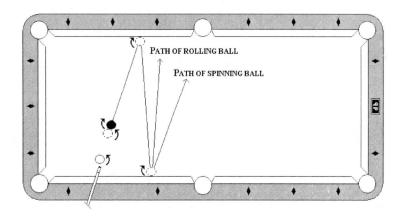

Figure 1-26 *Object ball reverses english*

But—ah, here I go again—that's the theory. The reality here is that most shots should not be hit hard enough for english on the object ball to carry past the first rebound. After that, the object ball will be rolling true—not spinning—so that it's approach angle and rebound angle will be the same.

So, unless you can control you stroke with meticulous accuracy, I recommend that most bank shots, if not all, be made using no side english. This way, the ball will always rebound at the same angle it approached the cushion. The *no english* approach to bank shots make them comparatively easy. However, there are three important reasons for using english. One is shape, two is to maneuver the object ball past another ball that would otherwise be in the way, and three (which is closely related to number two) is the ability to off-aim the object ball and still make the shot. But if you don't have to use english to make a bank shot, don't.

Winning Tip

If you don't have to use english to make a shot, don't.

There are no tricks or short cuts, so it's imperative that you understand the effects of english. Of course, the only way to thoroughly understand any of these english and angle principles is to practice, practice, practice and watch what happens.

If you really want to have fun, take notes. When I finally got down and dirty serious about the game, I filled a couple of notebooks with theories, possibilities, and trial outcomes of my practice sessions. It was an enormous help.

9. AIMING

Above all, a solid brick wall must be straight and true, and so must be your aim. The most difficult aspect of aiming, however, is trying to figure out what to aim at. Do you aim at the cue ball, the object ball, or the pocket? Although the cue must be stroked into the cue ball with precision, and, though the pocket is ultimately the target, neither is aimed at. The object ball, then, is the *object* of your aim. The cue ball must be aimed into the object ball, which will then travel (hopefully) to its intended target. Simple enough, except for one thing: the cue ball does not necessarily hit where it's aimed. In fact, there's only one shot in which the cue ball actually hits where it's aimed, and that's a straight in, full-face shot. You must aim at some place on the object ball other than the actual contact point to make all other shots.

So, aiming for some players is a matter of feel, which is learned by repetition (practice, practice, practice). For others, it's the use of tricks like imaginary lines, ghost balls, mirror tables, chalk marks on the cushion, sights or some other marks on the rail, or reflecting overhead lights on the balls. A few players even try to aim by using the side of the cue ball, and the side of the cue stick, instead of their centers.

For you, though, aiming can be a little more scientific than tricks. To begin with, looking down on the top of the object ball, think of it as a circle instead of a sphere. Technically, then, in 1° increments, there are 180° of directions from which the object ball can be struck: 90 on the right side and 90 on the left.

However, few players, if any, can aim at the ball with that kind of accuracy. Therefore, through the miracle of hundred year old technology, it's only necessary to think in terms of five contact points and, consequently, only five aiming points per side of a ball (Figure 1-27). Five. Can you dig it? And if you've spent your whole life thinking there were hundreds you're not alone.

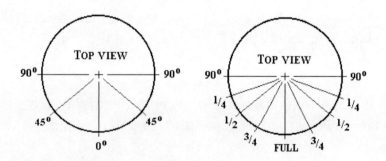

Figure 1-27 *Object ball contact points*

The five contact points are a full ball (0°), a $^1/_4$ ball, a $^1/_2$ ball (45°), a $^3/_4$ ball, and a 90° cut.

Can it be made any easier? You bet it can. The five aiming points for the object ball are also simple to find, even when thinking of a sphere instead of a circle. Figure 1-28 shows two views of a cue ball striking a 9 ball at each of the five contact points on the right side of the ball: the top view and the face view. The long arrow shows the aiming point and the shot arrow shows the contact point

Winning Tip

It is only necessary to think in terms of five aiming points per side of a ball: a full ball (0°), a $^1/_4$ ball, a $^1/_2$ ball (45°), a $^3/_4$ ball, and a 90° cut.

A full ball is aiming at, and hitting, the object ball full in the face (cue ball 1 in Figure 1-28). A $^1/_2$ ball is lined up by *aiming* the center of the cue ball at the outer edge of the object ball (cue ball 3 in Figure 1-28).

This is significant in that it gives you two aiming points that cannot be misjudged, and, from a learning standpoint, the $^1/_2$ ball aiming point is the most important because others are gauged *from* it.

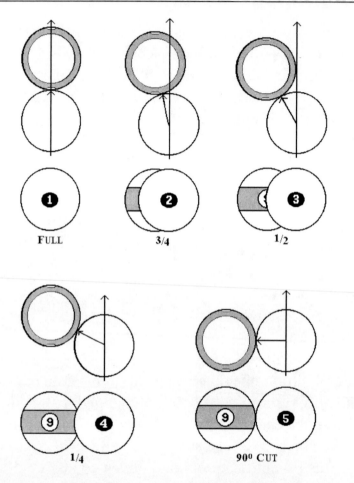

Figure 1-28 *Five aiming/contact points*

A 90° cut (although technically impossible, a good shooter can get close enough to make the shot) is made by striking the object ball at its outer edge (cue ball 5 in Figure 1-28). The aiming point is actually a half ball's width to the right (in this case) of the object ball.

Easier still, in essence, you only have to remember three contact points: Full, $^1/_2$, and 90° cut. The other two are found by interpolation. A $^3/_4$ ball is located halfway between the full ball and the $^1/_2$ ball (cue ball 2 in Figure 1-28). The $^1/_4$ ball is located halfway between the $^1/_2$ ball and the 90° cut (cue ball 4 in Figure 1-28).

Interpolation works something like this: When you're trying to make a shot similar to the one in Figure 1-29, lean over the table and aim for a 90° cut. Visualize it. Next, move the cue slightly and aim for the full-face ball. Visualize it. Notice that both shots will miss. However, if you aim anywhere between those two points, say a $^1/_2$ ball or so, you can't miss. Interpolation, then, is thinking in extremes—what will miss on one side and what will miss on the other side—then narrowing that down to what will make the shot.

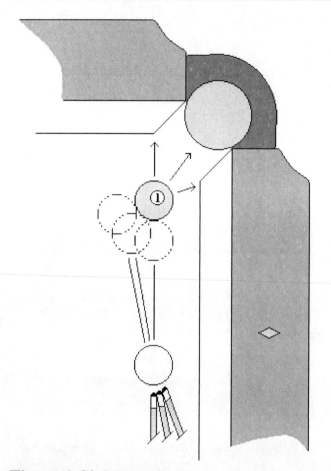

Figure 1-29 *Interpolation*

By using a little interpolation along with the five aiming points shown in Figure 1-28, most shots can be made. Of course, the example in Figure 1-29 is rather broad, but interpolation can be narrowed down. If the object ball is lined up so that two points of contact, say a $^3/_4$ ball and a $^1/_2$ ball isn't precise, then something between those can be used to make the shot, especially when a little english is added.

Practice hitting only these five contact points, it is much, much easier to think about hitting just $^1/_4$, $^1/_2$, or $^3/_4$ ball instead of hitting it at $^1/_3$ or $^2/_3$ or $^3/_8$ or $^{59}/_{64}$ or "about right there," or some other arbitrary point that could not be found again even with a laser sight. True story.

10. TABLE ROLL

   Table roll is a legitimate fundamental of the
game and must be mastered if you are going to win
consistently.

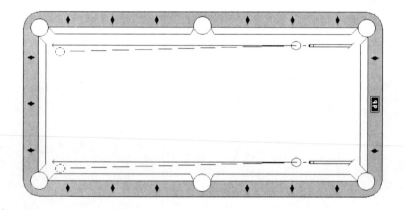

Figure 1-30 *Table roll*

   When a table rolls off you have two choices.
One, refuse to acknowledge that this is part of the
game, that the law of physic dictates that the ball
will roll toward the low side, and continue to miss
what would otherwise be easy shots. (Oh, and this
gives you an excuse to lose, after all "the table rolls
off.") Or two, simply use the roll-off to your
advantage.
   Always pay attention to the ball's drift,
especially when playing on an unfamiliar table. If

time permits, cue the cue ball up and down the table and note the roll-off (Figure 1-30).

Make a few shots taking the roll-off into account. If the table rolls left play the shot right or add a little right english to compensate, and let the ball drift into the pocket. It only takes a couple shots to get the feel of how much it rolls off. (And, who knows, it might even improve your golf game).

Winning Tip

Table roll is a legitimate fundamental of the game and must be mastered if you are going to win consistently.

The roll-off will not change from one shot to the next; it will remain the same until someone fixes the table. In other words, winning players will use the roll-off to their advantage.

Realistically, it is far easier to plan on, and be prepared to shoot on, a table that is not level than it is to count on one to be perfectly level.

SUMMARY

Bobby Knight, four-time NCAA winning basketball coach for Indiana University, had his players walk through their practice, each step laid out in slow motion like professional dancers choreographing their routines. This isn't a bad idea when practicing pool by yourself. Take each fundamental in slow deliberate steps. Teach yourself the right way, and correct any faults you already have.

Millions of people play pool every day. A large number learn some simple basics of the game, and no more. Others play their whole lives and learn only a small amount of the fundamentals, and a majority of those are obviously wrong. But only a few take those fundamentals to heart; to the point of learning to play seriously, and very few carry that through far enough to learn to play to win.

Learning to play to win means, fundamentally anyway, that you must play each and every game as if it's a tournament game. It may take some discipline to learn to play every shot as if it has some significance other than just wiling away the time, but that's what you have to be willing to do, every shot, every game.

When you recognize that every shot, despite who you're playing and where, is a must make shot, then you'll approach a time when you can play with the same intensity in every game and every circumstance.

In other words, if you don't let up when you're playing a so called friendly game the apprehension that comes with the pressure to perform won't be nearly as strong when you approach a tournament game, because you'll perceive it as just another game.

Pressure and anxiety are covered in more detail in chapter four. In the meantime, here's something to think about while you're practicing:

Don't take the fundamentals for granted.

Develop a good stance, it's your foundation.

Choose a cue that suites you and keep it maintained.

Be firm in your grip, but don't choke the cue, and keep it level when shooting.

Contort your fingers until your bridge works for you, not against you.

Don't duck the mechanical bridge, if you need it use it.

Stroking allows your body, eyes, and cue to be aligned for the shot.

Cue the ball with follow through; it's part of the cuing process.

There are only nine essential english cuing points, memorize them.

Position play is no great mystery. Anyone should be able to play excellent position shots with a minimal amount of practice.

Throw the ball to open the pocket, and know how inside and outside english affects the ball.

There are only five essential aiming and contact points, memorize those.

Remember table roll; it's a legitimate fundamental of the game.

And: Play every game to win, because there's no such thing as a friendly game, it's a fundamental of dirty pool.

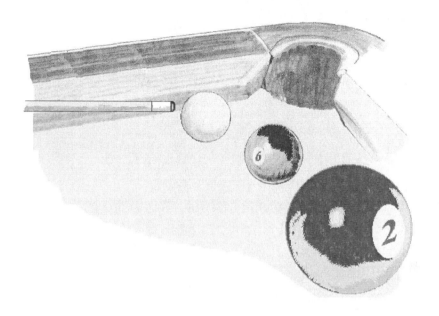

TEN WINNING PRACTICE SHOTS

Shot making adheres the fundamentals into a solid winning game as sure as mortar adheres the bricks to make a solid wall. And solid shot making comes with practice.

The legendary Minnesota Fats came to the grand opening of the Velvet Rail. He was there for three days and two nights of exhibition shooting.

Minnesota Fats was a gracious, rotund man with impeccable manners. During performances and public appearances, he insisted on wearing a sports coat and collared shirt, though not usually a tie. But on the road, he sometimes became unrecognizable, often looking quite the bum. If you didn't recognize him in front of a pool room, out of compassion, you might slip him a dollar of two, which he would gladly accept, needed or not. And if you gave him a chance on the tables inside, you'd give him the rest of your money, too.

Minnesota Fats was indoctrinated into the BCA hall of fame without winning a major tournament. BCA's reasoning was his lifetime contribution of promoting the game. He was a master. The game will miss him.

In public, Minnesota Fats insisted that he would only shoot for money and only if the stakes were for a thousand or more a game. But during the hours we spent shaking down the table he was to do his exhibition shooting on, he taught me a great deal about practicing, not only the ten practice shots listed here but also ball contact, over and under aiming, cloth roll, and of course, hustling. "You never get so good as to not practice the essentials," he told me.

Winning Tip

You never get so good as to not practice the essentials.

At first (or second or third) glance, you might think there are hundreds of shots that must be learned and practiced to cover "the essentials," and to become a winning pool player. Nope. The number, in reality, is a lot less. If you can master the following ten shots, you've got it made. All other shots are some variation of one or more of these.

These shots can be set up and practiced repeatedly, and should never be missed during a game. And if you never miss them, you'll win consistently. Rehearse them during practice sessions only, not while playing. Although learning from every shot made is important, learning while practicing, without outside influence, is invaluable.

Also, when it comes to shot making and winning, here is a handy rule of thumb I use for guidance: Any shot that involves more than two balls is a sucker shot. Once you include a third ball or a rail into the mix, the difficulty of the shot rises significantly, and your odds of winning decrease accordingly. Of course, that's a generalization because some three ball shots are easy duck shots and can be essential to winning a game, like a short, straight-in combination shot on the 9 ball. But usually, you should never

Winning Tip
Although learning from every shot made is important, learning while practicing, without outside influence, is invaluable.

bypass a two ball shot for any three ball or bank shot. And any four ball or two-rail bank shot should be relegated to trick shots, along with jump and massé shots.

Practicing by yourself is important, for sure. It also alleviates outside influence and the pressure to perform it can cause. But often it's worthwhile to have a practice partner, someone of equal or greater skills than yourself, someone who can tell you what you're doing right or wrong during a shot. This too can be invaluable. Just make sure your practice partner is as dedicated to learning and winning as you are.

Winning Tip

Often it's worthwhile to have a practice partner, just make sure your partner is as dedicated as you are.

1. ENGLISH—CUE BALL CONTROL SHOTS

Set an object ball and a cue ball on the table as illustrated in Figure 2-1. Using no english, strike the object ball at the $^1/_2$ ball point. Note that the object ball goes straight into the side pocket and the cue ball rebounds off the end rail at the same angle as it approached (C in Figure 2-1).

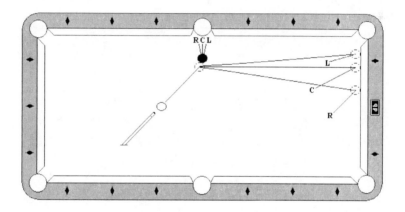

Figure 2-1 *English shot*

Repeat the shot using left english, then right english, and notice what happens to the object ball. Left english sends it slightly right and right english sends it slightly left.

Also notice what happens to the cue ball. Here, left english *opens* the angle of approach and *closes* the angle of rebound from the end rail, and right english *closes* the angle of approach and *opens* the angle of rebound. Practicing and understanding these english shots, using both side and corner pockets, are essential to learning to control the cue ball.

Further, with center english (follow, stop, or draw), the angle of rebound of the object ball will be equal to the angle of approach; that is, the angle coming off the rail will be the same as the angle going into the rail. Practice this shot from both sides of the table, hitting the object ball on the right side then the left, using $^3/_4$, $^1/_2$, and $^1/_4$ ball contact points.

In addition, since english and cue ball control work together, it's important that you practice both at the same time. So, using whatever english and object ball contact points deemed necessary, try to pocket a circle of eight, ten, or twelve balls, starting with the cue ball in the center (Figure 2-2). You can vary the diameter of the circle to suite different practice needs. This drill is excellent practice for draw (low) english.

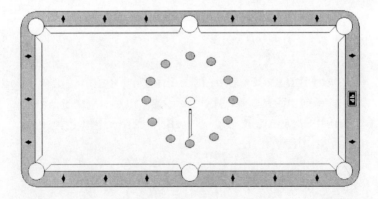

Figure 2-2 *Cue ball control*

2. STRAIGHT IN SHOTS

Straight in shots are often called the most difficult in pool when actually the shot is by far the easiest to make. Simply aim the full ball straight into the pocket and use either stop or draw english.

What's really meant by difficult in making a straight in shot is trying to make the shot without scratching or, even tougher, getting the cue ball into position for the next shot.

You can accomplish this by simply using any combination of side english and off aiming the object ball slightly. If you use right english, off aim to the right. If you use left english, off aim to the left. It works every time.

For practicing purposes, mimic Figure 2-3 by aligning the cue ball and object ball straight into a pocket, then off aim, use any side english, and a solid stroke. It couldn't be easier.

Cue Ball

Winning Tip

Off aim in the direction of the english. Left english, aim the object ball slightly left of the target. Right english, aim slightly right of the target.

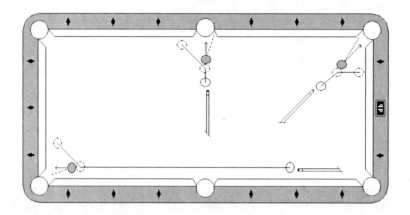

Figure 2-3 *Straight in shots*

Straight in shots remain relatively simple as long as the object ball is close to the cue ball. Inadvertent english has less time to take affect and the chances of unintentionally throwing the object ball away from the target is nil.

However, straight in shots become exponentially difficult as the distance between the cue ball, object ball, and pocket increases. Precise cue ball control becomes essential as these distances increase.

3. ANGLE SHOTS

If you think about an angle shot from the point of view of a straight in shot, then no matter what angle the shot is made from, you can use the straight-in contact point.

Winning Tip
Think of an angle shot from the point of view of a straight in shot

Set up an object ball and cue ball as illustrated in Figure 2-4 and practice from several angles. Using a $^1/_2$ ball shot, a full ball shot, and a 90° shot with no side english, strike the object ball at the same contact point each time and watch what happens. Try the shot using both left and right english, then try draw and follow. Remember to off aim the object ball.

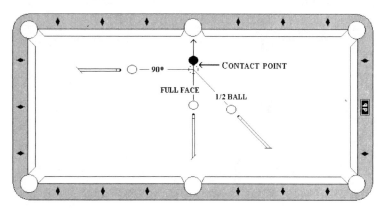

Figure 2-4 *Angle shots*

You should be able to make this shot from anywhere on the table using any english. When practicing, walk around the table and decide where the cue ball would contact the object ball to send it straight into a pocket, using the correct aiming point.

Ideally, when you're playing, you want to be able to perceptively visualize your aiming and contact points. If you want to mark the table or rail during practice, that's fine. But during the game, leave that silliness to the part-timers.

4. RAIL SHOTS

Set an object ball dead against a rail, and a cue
ball at some angle behind the object ball but away
from the rail, as illustrated in Figure 2-5.

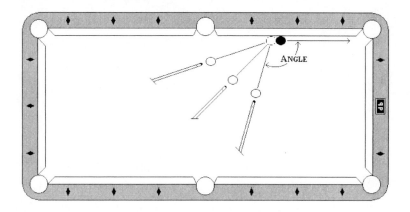

Figure 2-5 *Rail shots*

Play the object ball down the rail into a corner
pocket. Because the object ball is resting on the rail,
it's hard to visualize the necessary aiming point,
especially as the angle of the cue ball, in relation to
the object ball, decreases. But if you remember the
angle shot and visualize the rail shot as if it were
straight in, as if you were using a full-face ball
instead of, say a $^1/_4$ ball, it seems to be a little easier.

First, use no side english and strike the object ball
and the cushion at the same time. Then try the shot

using different english and be aware of what happens to both the cue ball and object ball. In this case (Figure 2-5), left (outside) english is the better shot. It forces the object ball to roll along the cushion.

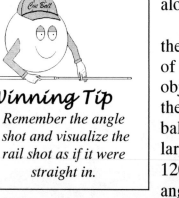

Winning Tip

Remember the angle shot and visualize the rail shot as if it were straight in.

Some players insist that they hit the rail a fraction of an inch before hitting the object ball. This works if the angle between the cue ball and the object ball is large, somewhere around 120° or more. But as the angle decreases to around 70° or less, it becomes more and more difficult. The best course is to always hit both at the same time and use slight outside english.

The rail shot is one of those shots that become excruciatingly easy with a little practice. You should be able to make it, every time.

5. SPOT SHOTS

Set an object ball on the foot spot and place the cue ball behind the head string close to a side rail (Figure 2-6). The "spot shot" is a basic shot that should never be missed. Practice it until it can be made from either side of the table without scratching. Try using a $^1/_4$ ball contact point and no side english with a moderate stroke, then try

Winning Tip

The spot shot is a basic shot that should be made every time.

different english and contact points and note what happens to the cue ball.

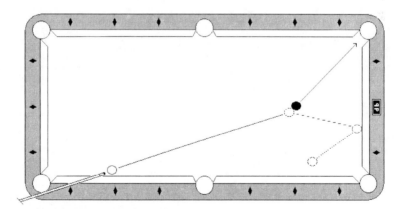

Figure 2-6 *Spot shots*

If your opponent scratches while making the key ball thinking he or she is playing safe because the spot shot is one of the toughest possible, you'll set him or her on fire because you won't miss. Right?

6. FROZEN BALL SHOTS

When struck, two object balls frozen together (touching), can take three paths.

First, the first object ball that the cue ball strikes will travel at right angles from the centerline created by the two frozen balls, and away from the cue ball (ball 1 in Figure 2-7). Second, the second object ball (ball 2 in Figure 2-7) will travel away from the first along the centerline. Third, the second object ball can be "thrown" off that centerline, if desired.

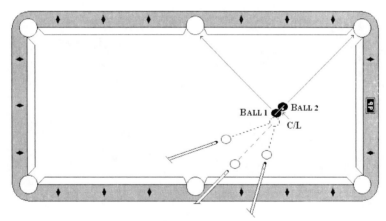

Figure 2-7 *Frozen ball shots*

In this setup, shooting in a left to right order, the cue ball should hit the first object ball at the $^3/_4$, $^1/_2$, and full face contact points. The first object ball is made into the side pocket and the second in the corner pocket. Except for cue ball placement, side english will not affect the shot.

Of course, the balls are not always conveniently lined up as in Figure 2-7. Figure 2-8 illustrates the second object ball being thrown off the centerline and into a corner pocket. To make this shot, use no side english, strike the first object ball on the opposite side of the direction of the throw. The amount of throw depends on the crispness of your stroke and the distance to a pocket.

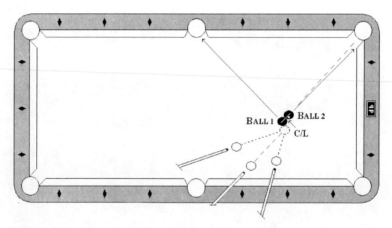

Figure 2-8 *Frozen object ball throw shots*

Although this shot is not particularly hard, it is one that should only be played if no other shot is available, ball 1 being your next object ball, or if the cluster must be broken up, for example. Ideally, though, you would make some other ball and use the cue ball to break these two apart, and maybe still make one, or both.

Further, and more important, is a shot in which one of the two frozen balls is the cue ball. I say more important because, unless you can shoot away from the frozen ball at some other object ball, this shot has to be taken. In this case, the object ball can also be

Winning Tip
At first, throw shots will seem impossible, but after some practice, they will become routine.

played along the centerline of the two balls or it can be slightly thrown off the line.

If the balls are aligned with the pocket (ball 1 in Figure 2-9) it is easily made with stop or draw english, though you may not get the shape you want. An alternative is to throw the object ball into the pocket and gain control over the cue ball.

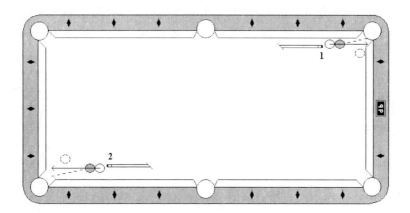

Figure 2-9 *Frozen cue ball throw shots*

Another useful throw shot situation is if the balls are a little out of alignment with the pocket (ball 2 in Figure 2-9). In this case, the object ball *must* be thrown into its target, if it's to be made.

In both cases, a full cue tip's diameter of draw english must be applied to the opposite side of the direction of the desired throw.

Set these shots up in various places around the table and practice them. At first they might seem impossible, but after some practice they will become routine.

7. BANK AND KICK SHOTS

A bank shot occurs when the object ball rebounds off one or more cushions into a pocket or another object ball. A kick shot also involves a bank, but the cue ball rebounds from the cushion first and then into the object ball.

Playing your shot into a cushion is a little tricky in that, unless you're shooting straight on, the ball does not contact the cushion at your aiming point (Figure 2-10). But that's not a problem as long as you always aim for the sight (or other target) and not worry about where the ball actually makes contact.

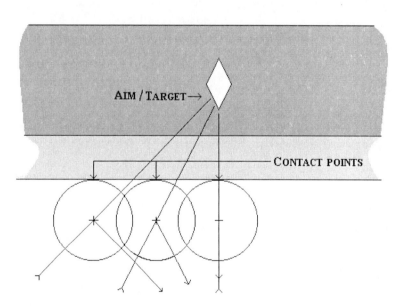

Figure 2-10 *Target the sight*

I've known players who always tried to imagine a line running from the target perpendicularly into the cushion nose, then tried to contact the rail at that point, and added side english to compensate for the angle. This may at first seem like the easy way to plot a bank shot, and players who can control their english well, do become fairly adept at banking this way.

However, the surest way is to simply shoot directly at your target with no side english, because it's easy to remember that a ball with no side english rebounds from the cushion at the same angle it approaches.

Winning Tip

Unless you're shooting straight on, the ball does not contact the cushion at your aiming point.

All shots depicted in Figures 2-11 and 2-12 are simple, across the table bank shots, and are the only ones needed to play winning pool. They should, however, be thoroughly practiced before you use them in a game. Long bank shots, those played from one end of the table to the other, are more difficult and should be practiced, but they should be used only when necessary. Complicated bank shots, like double banks and around the table banks, should never be used in a serious game. I know: never say never, but you know what I mean.

Simple Bank Shots

There have been countless theories and diagrams explaining ways to make simple bank shots. Some involve shooting into pockets on phantom pool tables out in never, never land; some suggest shooting at mirrors; and others take you deep into geometric formulas ($(\sqrt{a^2 + b^2}) = c$) and (the base angles of an isosceles triangle are equal, as are the legs). But we already know that, right? So, without going any deeper into the mathematics of basic geometry, just bear in mind that opposite sides of squares and rectangles (or a pool table) are equal, and that's what makes simple bank shots simple.

In pool table terms, then, if you have a ball at pocket C and want to bank it into pocket B, as in Figure 2-11, because pockets C and B are on the ends of one side of a square (rail 6 in this case), you can target the opposite side (rail 2) in the middle, and make the ball, as long as you use no side english. Further, any object ball lying on that line can be made into objective pocket B by hitting the same target.

To find the middle of the opposite side, take its length and divide by two. This is fairly simple on a pool table because the rails are already divided into four equal spaces that link pockets and sights.

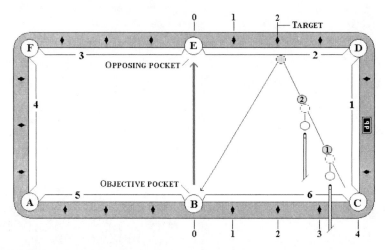

Figure 2-11 *Simple bank shots*

In Figure 2-11, object balls 1 and 2 are both on a line that represents an angle of approach that begins four spaces from objective pocket B. The line ends at the second sight (or two spaces) from the opposing pocket on the opposite rail. This point is the target. The angle of rebound line starts at the target and ends at the objective pocket.

This works no matter where the angle of approach line begins. To locate the target, simply count the sights (or

Winning Tip

To locate the target, simply count the sights from the objective pocket to the beginning of the approach line and divide by two.

spaces) from the objective pocket to the beginning
of the angle of approach line that your object ball
lies on and divide by two.

In Figure 2-12, look at each object ball and its
path one at a time. Object ball 1 is the same as in
Figure 2-11 and was left for reference, but to
review: Pocket C is four sights (or spaces) from
pocket B, the objective pocket; and the target is two
sights from pocket E, the opposing pocket (4 ÷ 2).

Object ball 2 is on a line that connects the third
sight from objective pocket B and its target at one
and a half sights from opposing pocket E on the
opposite rail (3 ÷ 2).

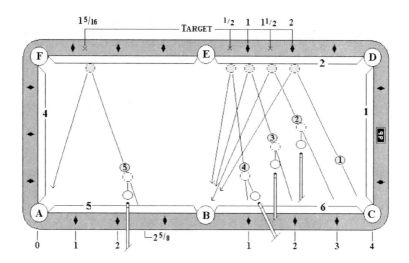

Figure 2-12 *More simple bank shots*

Object ball 3 is on a line that connects the second sight from pocket B and its target at the first sight from opposing pocket E (2 ÷ 2).

Object ball 4 is on a line that connects the first sight from its objective pocket and its target, half a sight from the opposing pocket (1 ÷ 2).

Figuring out the locations of any angle of approach line or target can be accomplished quickly by visualizing a line that starts at some point on the first rail, passes through the object ball, and ends at the target on the opposite rail.

You can use a little interpolation to narrow the range when the object ball isn't lying on a line conveniently aligned between two sights. If you misjudge your starting point by thinking ball 5 in Figures 2-12 and 2-13 is at the third sight, for example, your target would be the one and a half sights on the opposite rail (3 ÷ 2). But that line *doesn't* come close to passing through the object ball (dashed line in Figure 2-13). So, you have to move the line until the math works as it passes through the object ball.

You can practice finding the approach line, and target of various shots by laying your cue across the table, on top of the object ball, with the tip toward the opposite rail, then, using the object ball as a pivot point, rotate the cue until the tip is half the distance from the opposing pocket as the butt is from the objective pocket. After a little practice,

targets will become conspicuously visible without
the cue. And, as you become proficient, you won't
even have to do the calculations, you'll just see the
target.

Object ball 5 in Figures 2-12 and 2-13 is
actually lying on a line that begins two and five-
eights sights from objective pocket A and ends one
and five-sixteenths sights from opposing pocket F
($2^5/_8 \div 2$). But that's getting a little carried away.

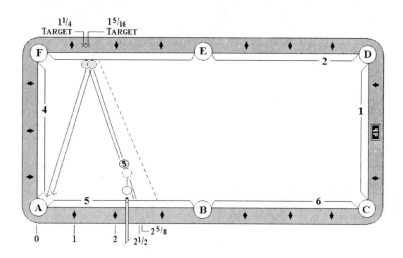

Figure 2-13 *Bank shots*

These fractions could go on and on until they're
so far out of hand that we're back to complicating
something that's supposed to be simple. But once
you recognize their relationship to each other, and

the leeway you have in making a bank shot, you can forget most of the fractions altogether.

On a standard pool table, the usable part of a pocket opening is roughly two and a quarter inches; that is, you can deviate an inch and an eighth on either side of the pocket opening's centerline and still make the shot (Figure 2-14). Or, since the number is halved on the opposite rail, you can off play the target by half an inch or so and still be okay.

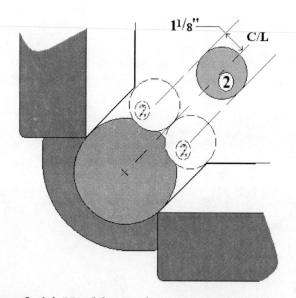

Figure 2-14 *Usable pocket opening*

The significance of this deviation is that you only have to divide the spaces between the rail sights into fourths (¼, ½, ¾, 1, etc.), eliminating all other mind muddling fraction possibilities. If, for example, the approach line actually lays two and five-eights sights from its objective pocket (ball 5 in Figures 2-12 and 2-13), you could safely call it two and a half sights, play a one and a quarter target on the opposite rail, and make the shot; making simple bank shots even simpler.

Further, and something else to keep in mind, long bank shots, from one end of the table to the other, are visualized the same as across the table shots. At first glance, you might think that the opposite rail would be quartered instead of halved, since the table is twice as long as it is wide. But remember, opposite sides are equal on a rectangle, as well as a square. So, for example, if you wanted to bank a ball lying at one corner pocket into the adjacent corner pocket at the same end of the table, simply target the opposite rail in the middle. Etcetera. Etcetera. Etcetera.

Kick Shots

Kick shots can also be simple, easy shots like shot 1 in Figure 2-15, or they can be extremely hard like shots 2 and 3.

A kick shot is similar to a bank shot in that a cushion is involved, but here, the cue ball rebounds from a cushion before hitting the object ball. Unlike a bank shot, though, your aiming point is the rail and your target is the object ball. But you can find your aiming point exactly as if you were finding the target point in a bank shot.

Easy kick shots can be played with abandon because they are actually hard to miss (shot 1 in Figure 2-15, for example), and in some cases can't be missed, even if you fail to see your target points precisely, because the object balls are usually trapped in the jaws of a pockets. That's what makes them easy!

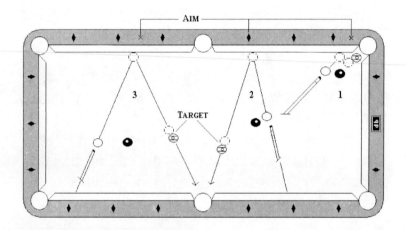

Figure 2-15 *Kick shots*

Hard kick shots, on the other hand—and unlike bank shots—can be missed by inches simply by miscalculating the aiming and target points by meager fractions, and, therefore, should be ignored if at all possible, like all complicated bank shots.

8. CAROM AND KISS SHOTS

Carom shots occur when the cue ball strikes one object ball then careens or glances into another object ball. Kiss shots are similar except the object ball strikes another ball before continuing on. These shots are extremely valuable when playing

Winning Tip

Carom and kiss shots are extremely valuable when playing Nine Ball.

Nine Ball, and not really that difficult when the balls are in close proximity to each other (Figure 2-16).

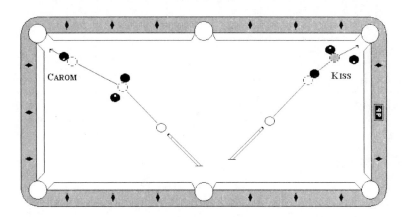

Figure 2-16 *Carom and Kiss shots*

Both shots become exceptionally difficult and change drastically, though, with the use of english and as the balls get farther apart. Practice a few shots like the ones shown in Figure 2-16, and use them to your advantage. Also, play both of these shots with little or no side english, and use some follow to help drive the cue ball. But, remember, these shots involve more than two balls, so, unless absolutely necessary, try not to use either of them if there's a lot of green between the two object balls.

I know, I know: here's a difficult shot, practice it until you're blue in the face, but don't use it in a game. I'm starting to sound like a broken record (as the saying goes). But ignoring hard shots is the winning way because you want each shot to be as uncomplicated as possible. Remember what I said earlier: If all shots are easy, straight in shots, you can't lose.

So why spend time practicing tough shots, if you're going to ignore them? Well, they can't always be ignored. Sometimes you'll have to play the hardest, dumbest shot on the table, because it'll be the only one available to you. Your chances of making the shot goes up immeasurably if you're aware of how it works and how to make it. Practice all the hard shots you can, know them inside and out, but don't use them in a game unless you absolutely have to.

9. COMBINATION SHOTS

A combination shot occurs when the object ball strikes another object ball forcing the second ball into a pocket or intended target (Figure 2-17).

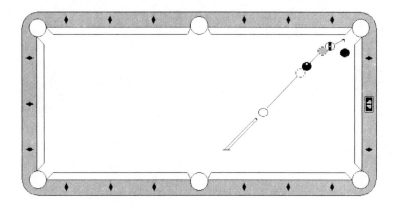

Figure 2-17 *Combination shots*

A few years ago, I would have said that this shot (like any shot involving more than two balls) should be avoided except on extreme, no other shot available, situations. However, because of the popularity of Nine Ball, this shot has become passionately

Winning Tip
Because of Nine Ball, combinations shots have become passionately necessary and should be learned in depth.

necessary and should be learned in depth, especially
if the balls are close together. Set up a few shots as
illustrated in Figure 2-17 and try them using various
english and ball contact points. Naturally, if you plan
on winning, I think *no* side english is better.

Like all three ball shots, combinations are
relatively simple as long as the object ball is close to
the cue ball. Unplanned english has less time to take,
and the chances of inadvertently throwing the object
ball from its target is zilch. However, combination
shots become more difficult as the distance between
the cue ball, object ball, and pocket increases, and
precise cue ball control becomes essential. As usual, a
shot like the one shown in Figure 2-18 should only be
attempted in a game if no other shot is available.

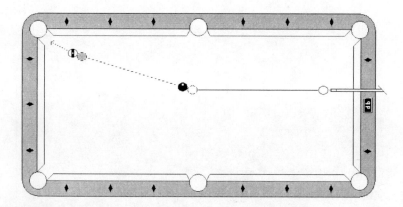

Figure 2-18 *Long combination shots*

10. LONG SHOTS

Long shots, even simple two ball long shots, can be disastrous. They are low percentage shots that, unfortunately, must often be played. If a long shot is the only one available, use follow english solely.

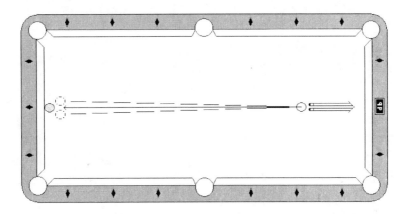

Figure 2-19 *Long shot cue ball drift*

Using side english, even the smallest amount, will cause the cue ball to "drift" away from its target. A cue tip's diameter of side english could send the cue ball off course as much as a ball's width over the length of the table, depending on cloth condition, size of the table, and how hard the cue ball is struck. So, along with english drift, table roll and cloth roll must also be accounted for.

Set up the long shot illustrated in Figure 2-19 and watch what happens. Set the shot up going both directions.

Winning Tip

Most shots change dramatically when the cue ball is setting at the opposite end of the table from the object ball.

Because long shots can't always be avoided, all shots—straight in shots, bank shots, cut shots, combination shots, etc.—must be practiced and mastered as long shots. These shots change dramatically when the cue ball is setting at the opposite end of the table from the object ball. Set up a variety of shots like those shown in Figure 2-20 and practice them using follow english only.

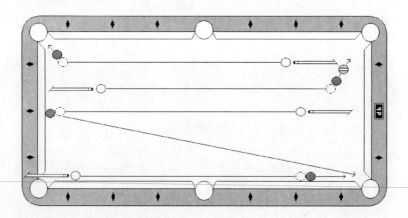

Figure 2-20 *Long shots*

Contrary to any intuitive felling you might have, long shots should be played with finesse, don't blast away just because the table suddenly looks like the 18th green at your city golf course.

When playing a long shot, unless the cue ball is struck extremely hand, english can take and dissipate long before contact is made with the object ball. Because of this, throw shots are virtually impossible, and combination shots, kick shots, kiss shots, or any other shot involving more than two balls become almost luck shots, or certainly extremely low percentage shots.

Winning Tip
If you want to win, keep your shot selection simple.

If you have to get lucky to win, you aren't playing winning pool, and anytime you play a shot that may or may not go in, you're playing luck pool. You've heard the old saying, I'd rather be lucky than good. I say it all the time. But I don't believe it, not for a second. Occasionally it's necessary to take a chance, but if you do it too often, you'll ultimately loose.

SUMMARY

Outside english opens the angle of approach and closes the angle of rebound from the rail. Inside english closes the angle of approach and opens the angle of rebound.

Straight in shots are made by simply aiming the full ball straight into the pocket and using either stop or draw english. Or you can throw the ball by off aiming in the direction of the english.

Often it's necessary to think about angle shots and rail shots from the point of view of a straight in shot.

Spot shots are made using no side english and a quarter ball aiming point.

It usually requires a full cue tip's diameter of side english to the opposite side of the direction of a desired throw shot.

When banking, if your target is a sight, aim directly at the sight. And, although carom, kiss, and combination shots have become popular, and often essential because of Nine Ball, they should be used in moderation.

If a long shot is the only one presented, use follow english exclusively. The greater the distance between the object ball, the cue ball, and the pocket, the more difficult the shot becomes. Keep your shot selection simple. Don't play a combination shot or carom shot when a simple cut shot will do the trick. More often than not, playing a safe or safety shot is a better choice over a low percentage shot.

TEN WINNING EIGHT BALL
AND NINE BALL STRATEGIES

I recently read that hustling or "sharking" went out with the nineteen-fifties because tournaments now pay enough to draw top players away from such endeavors. I think this is far from the truth. Top players—Greenleaf, Hoppe, Mosconi, Rambow, Caras—of days gone by always played in recognized tournaments of their time, as do top players of today. How else would we know their names? Top players will always play in

tournaments, and few, if any, will be hustlers.
Fame is far more appealing than dollars, especially
hustling for dollars in bars and poolrooms. Earl
Strickland (5 time US Open Nine Ball Champion)
is credited with saying, "I would have rather won
the tournament than the million dollars because I
play for pride. . . ."

Okay.

Furthermore, how many *top players* are there at
any given time? Twenty? Thirty? Fifty? Ten? How
many can you name?

Then there are a few, maybe a hundred or so,
who are fodder for the top players. After all, top
players have to beat someone. Fodder players are
excellent players, but they lack that small
something—attitude, natural skill, luck, good looks,
whatever—that it takes to become a Mizerak,
Strickland, Fisher, Lee, Corr, or newcomers like
Putnam or Deuel of our time. Who are these fodder
players? Where do they play at night? How do they
feed their own devotion to the game, besides
loosing to the top players?

And what about the rest of us, the thousands
and thousands who play good, or even excellent,
pool and think we could beat the best if only we
had the time or opportunity or bankroll. We're the
pool hall junkies and we don't play for fame or

recognition. We hustle for beers and dollars, and, even though we'll never be "top players," we play to win.

Bars and poolrooms have tried to clean up their images with leagues and tournaments, but—although it may be a little more covert then it was—hustling pool is still alive and well. That's all right though, because once pool becomes as sterile as a church social, like sanctioned tournaments or televised matches, it'll be about as much fun.

When I owned the Velvet Rail, a local hustler named "Rabbit" came in and played or practiced almost daily. I've seen him beat players who were far superior to him in their shooting abilities because he could always figure out a subtle way to take them out of their games. It's called sharking, and he was one of the great whites I've known. Mid morning one beautiful fall day, I was sitting at the food counter drinking coffee and watching a game between Rabbit and a black road player named Berry (affectionately called "Blackberry") from Louisville. Rabbit sauntered up to the counter, sat beside me, and ordered something to eat.

"How can you eat at a time like this?" I asked, and pointed to Berry. "He isn't missing a shot and you'll soon be broke."

"He's subject to start missing in a game or two and won't even know why," Rabbit slowly replied.

"Oh?" He had my attention.

"Because he's a show-off shooter, sub-consciously he'll start thinking that I'm not interested in the game or how he shoots, especially how he shoots. That'll slowly take him out of his game. Then I'll raise the stakes and blow his doors off."

Sure enough, after five or six games, Berry was dogging easy shots and trying to make low percentage shots just to prove how good he was.

When it was over, Rabbit had it all, including a new Viking cue Barry had just procured from Gordon Hart—founder of Viking Cue Manufacturing—himself.

I'm not necessarily advocating that you should hustle the game like Rabbit, or any road player for that matter. What I am advocating is that you begin playing like winner; that is, *playing to win*. Every game. Game after game. And that you start thinking like a hustler—*dirty pool*—so you too can start winning like one.

The only thing that has changed since the nineteen-fifties is the games themselves. Where it used to be One-pocket and Bank, now it's Eight Ball and Nine Ball because these are today's most popular league and tournament games. Also, because of their popularity, I have chosen to use only elements and strategies of Eight Ball and Nine Ball games in this chapter; however, these strategies can be applied to any other pool or cue game.

All game rules vary greatly from country to country and certainly from state to state within the United States, so it's important to establish or clarify "house rules" before any game begins.

House rules are established for various reasons from obstructions around the table, to the house not knowing or understanding the newest adaptations of the preferred rules. House rules, or any rules for that matter, are supposedly fair for everyone, but that's not always the case, and usually some changes—requiring all shots to be called, including caroms, kisses, banks, pockets, etc.—doesn't necessarily add to the skill or pleasure of the game, only it's length. Knowing the rules of the house will no doubt cut down on the possibility of an argument, of course, but you also need to know them so you can exploit them to your advantage. The player who is aware of the rules and how they affect the game has an enormous advantage when they do change, even if that change is slight.

That's *playing to win*, and, like building our metaphorical brick wall, you must think and plan ahead if you want your game to stand the pressure of its environment day in and day out. And you must learn to think in terms of using the rules and nuances of the game to your favor.

You must think, *dirty pool*, even though it's not really dirty, or cheating, or dishonest, but part of the game—an expected part of the game.

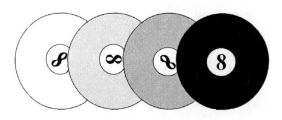

EIGHT BALL

Eight Ball is the most popular game in the United States and possibly in the world. It's played daily in bars, poolrooms, clubs, colleges, parks, recreation centers, retirement centers, and of course, homes. Youngsters barely old enough to hold a stick, up to oldsters barely young enough to hold a stick, play the game. It's enjoyed by all of them, and winnable by any of them.

The rules of Eight Ball take on many forms: shots that win under some rules, lose under others, and so forth. So, variations of rules must be declared before the game starts, and you have to know what they are and how they affect the game. The Billiard Congress of America's (BCA) Official Rules and Records book is the best place to start. If you haven't read it lately, it's time. The changes will surprise you.

Or try www.phoenixbilliards.com.

1. GAME OBJECTIVE

The team or player to legally pocket the 8 ball after all seven balls of a chosen group (stripes or solids) has been pocketed, wins the game. Sounds simple, right? Make eight balls and win.

Strategy

But the thing is, it doesn't matter if it takes eight shots or sixteen or a hundred to make those eight

Winning Tip

If you can't make your shot, or, if you can make it but can't get shape for the next ball, then don't even try. Play a safety.

balls. What counts is that you legally make the 8 ball before your opponent, which differs from some games where every ball or ball value is scored. This makes Eight Ball as much a defensive game as it is offensive, but most players seem to refuse to let this little fact sink in, and they blast away at unmakable shots, or setting ducks that if made actually give their opponents the advantage. So, if you can't make your shot, or, if you can make it but can't get shape for the next ball, then don't even try. A valiant attempt in this game will cost you more than it'll pay you. Simply play a defensive safe or safety shot and try your best to leave your opponents with difficult shots. Let them blast away. If you always leave them hooked, it'll soon erode their games. They'll start taking chances and trying luck or low percentage shots, leaving you with a wide open table. Be patient.

2. GAME PROCEDURE

Rack all fifteen balls with the 8 ball in the front center of the triangle, any ball on the front apex, a stripe ball on one rear apex, and a solid ball on the other rear apex (Figure 3-1). The other balls can be randomly racked.

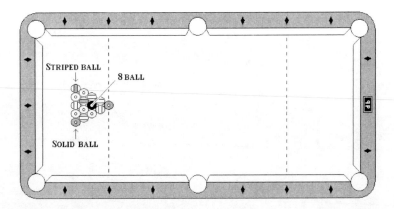

Figure 3-1 *Eight Ball rack*

Strategy One

In some cases, rules specify that the balls be racked alternately—stripe, solid, stripe, solid —around the triangle. The problem with this is it always leaves a ball of the same group on the three apexes of the rack. This rule usually stipulates that the 1 ball must also be placed on the front apex, which insures that all apex balls are solids.

Like a lot of subtleties of pool, just being aware of this gives you a slight advantage because the solids are more exposed to the break, and will usually scatter more than the stripes.

Strategy Two

A legal shot occurs when you shoot any ball in your group first, pocketing it or any other ball in your group, or sending it, any other object ball, or the cue ball to a rail.

This allows you to make defensive safe shots after defensive safe shots. A defensive safe shot is simply a planned miss. Except for loss of turn, there is no penalty for missing

Winning Tip

There's no penalty for playing defensive safe shots, as long as you make a legal shot.

because missing is not a foul, as long as you make a legal shot as described above. This is a dream come true for a patient player out to win. Just make sure that when you miss, you leave your opponent hooked or at least with a tough shot.

A deliberate miss is not a safety, so they don't have to be declared. Safeties are covered in more detail later.

Strategy Three

The general rule is that only ball and pocket must be called and only if they are not obvious. It isn't necessary to call the number of banks, kisses, carom, etc. A variation of Eight Ball is that all balls, including the 8 ball, must be called, combinations, kicks, kisses, caroms, bank shots, and pockets must be stated, and some rules even want cushion shots called; that is, if you run a ball down a rail, you must state how many times it's going to contact that rail. I know, I know: dumb. But I don't make these wacky, off-the-wall rules.

This is one of those variations of rules that do nothing for the game except drag it out, and it doesn't necessarily favor the better shooter. It can, however, favor the smarter player, the one with the most patience—you. This variation also makes the game a safe player's paradise because your opponents must also call the exact tracks of their balls, so its easier for you to leave them with a hard shot. If they insist that this variation be enforced, simply try to leave them hooked. Shot after shot. It won't take long to break their spirit.

Of course, you don't want to announce that this is your strategy. Just do it.

3. THE BREAK

The order of the break is usually determined by lot, lag, or coin toss. During a break, you have the cue ball in-hand behind the head string. Your break must pocket a ball or send at least four object balls to a rail, but the idea is to make as many balls as possible, hopefully all from the same group.

Strategy One
Some rules dictate that you break by hitting the apex ball first. In this case, place the cue ball on the head spot and hit the rack head-on using slightly high, driving english (Figure 3-2).

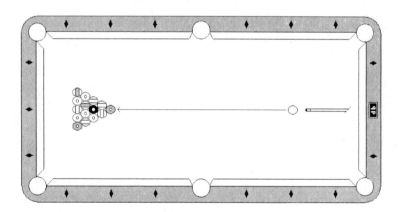

Figure 3-2 *Eight Ball head-on break*

High english forces the cue ball through the breaking rack after its initial hit, helping to scatter the balls.

Strategy Two

More than likely, the rule will allow you to hit the rack anywhere. In this case, place the cue ball four to eight inches off either side rail, aim for a solid hit on the second ball in the rack, and use low english to draw the cue ball away from a possible scratch in the corner pocket (Figure 3-3). Hit the shot firmly, but not as hard as the apex ball break. This will also effectively scatter the rack, giving you the best possibility of making a ball or two after the break, and continuing to shoot.

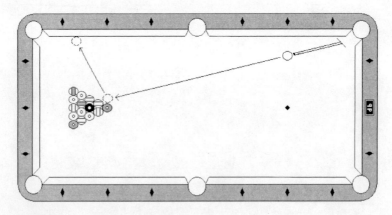

Figure 3-3 *Eight ball side break*

Strategy Three

Most rules say that making the 8 ball on the break is not a win or loss, it is simply spotted and play continues.

More often than not, though, and certainly for coin-operated tables, if the 8 ball is pocketed on the break, it is either a win or loss of the game. This rule *must* be determined before the start of the game.

If the 8 ball loses on the break, a soft break might be your strategy, trying not to roll the 8 ball far.

If the 8 ball wins on the break, go for it. Just don't scratch.

Strategy Four

If your opponent breaks and an object ball leaves the table, you have the choice of either accepting the balls as they lie, or taking the cue ball in-hand within the balk area and shooting from there.

Look the table over carefully. Remember, it's still open and, because the jumped ball is not spotted, one ball has been made. And you also have a choice of where to start shooting from. This could be an enormous advantage for you.

4. AFTER THE BREAK

Your break must pocket a ball or send at least four object balls to a rail. If this does not occur, your opponent can accept the balls as they lie and choose which group to shoot, re-break a new rack, or have you re-break a new rack. If you pocket any object ball on the break, the table is still open and you have the choice of which group to shoot.

Strategy One

No matter how many balls you make on the break or from what group, you still have the *choice* of which group to shoot. Choose the color group that has the least clusters, or has the best arrangement of balls for a possible run, in other words, choose the group that offers the best winning possibilities. Don't choose a group simply because one or two balls of that group have been made.

Winning Tip

No matter how many balls you make on the break or from what group, you have the choice of which group to shoot.

Strategy Two

When the table is open, you can shoot any ball, to make another. Playing a solid into a stripe to make the stripe, for example, is legal.

Some rules consider hitting the 8 ball first as a foul, others consider it legal, and some rules stipulate that the 8 ball can be used in a combination shot, as long as it's not the first to be hit. Usually, though, if these shots are legal, they're only legal if the table is open. So, don't overlook them.

Winning Tip

Knowing obscure and often ignored rules opens up a variety of possible shots that might otherwise be missed.

Knowing obscure and often ignored rules opens up a variety of possible shots that might otherwise be missed.

Strategy Three

Scratching on the break is a foul, but not a loss of game. Your opponent gets the cue ball in-hand behind the head string, but cannot directly shoot at balls lying within the balk area (the area behind the head string). But the table is open no matter how many balls you made, or from which group. So, if you made three solids on the break and scratched, you've given your opponent an enormous advantage. If you don't scratch, though, you've given yourself an enormous advantage. Use one of the two breaks shown above to insure a good break, *without scratching*. Don't give up any advantage unnecessarily.

Strategy Four

To win, you have to make eight balls. If, after you break, the balls are arranged in such a way that allows you a winning run, that's great. But, if you can't run all eight balls for the win, run as many as you can then play a defensive safe or safety shot, and try to leave your opponent without a shot. If you want to impress the crowd, go ahead and try the three-cushion kiss shot or the three-ball combo. But, if you want to win, play safe.

"D-fence! D-fence!" you've heard and seen it a thousand times in pro sports. There's nothing wrong with playing defense. Leave the macho shooting to your opponent.

Some players find making safe shots difficult. They are. Often it's easier—and less embarrassing —for them to miss a low percentage shot than it is to make a good safe or safety. You gotta love those players. Just don't be one of them.

Strategy Five

If your opponent fails to make a legal break (fails to pocket a ball or send at least four balls to a rail), you have the option of playing the balls as they lie, re-racking and re-breaking, or having your opponent re-break a new rack.

Don't be rash in your assessment of the table. Look for an easy run out before making your decision. If you decide to re-rack in a game in which the 8 ball wins on the break, give it your best break shot. If the 8 ball looses on the break, consider your opponent's ability to run eight balls. You might be wise to give up the re-break.

Winning Tip

Don't be rash in your assessment of the table. You might be wise to give up any re-break.

5. PATTERNS

Some players consider shot making sequence, lay of the table, and patterns as the same thing. But there are some differences. Sequence is the order in which you shoot or will shoot the balls. Lay of the table is the way the balls are distributed on the table after each shot. After some practice, a good eye will began to see repeating groupings and sameness of the lay of the table. These groupings become patterns, and once you become more astute at recognizing these patterns you will automatically know which balls to shoot and in what sequence (Figure 3-4).

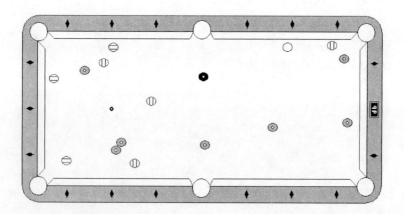

Figure 3-4 *Lay of the table*

Strategy One

After the break, carefully look at the lay of the table. Within it you'll find a couple of straight-in shots, a couple of combination shots, a bank shot or two, and maybe a carom or kiss shot possibility. If you were to break the rack a hundred times, although the balls will lie slightly different, these same patterns will stand out.

Go ahead, break a few racks, and notice how the balls scatter, or, more importantly, where they settle. Don't shoot any balls, just re-rack and re-break. Break both hard and soft, and watch the same patterns develop, time and again.

Once you can scan the table and recognize these patterns, you are well on your way to planning a sequence of shots that will allow you to win.

Strategy Two

Since you only need eight shots to win, plan your sequence by starting with the 8 ball and working backward. This will quickly tell you how many clusters must be dealt with, if you have to play a safe,

Winning Tip

Plan your sequence by starting with the 8 ball and working backward.

and, if so, where? Once a shot has been missed, or your opponent has taken a shot or two, you have to reassess because of course the lay of the table will change, as will the patterns, and therefore, so must your sequence. To reassess, you must, again, start with the 8 ball and work backward.

Strategy Three

Solids in Figure 3-4 look good, all spread out except for two balls clustered together at the left foot of the table. Stripes, on the other hand, seem more constricted at first glance, but if you plan the sequence carefully, there's nothing stopping a run out with them (Figure 3-5).

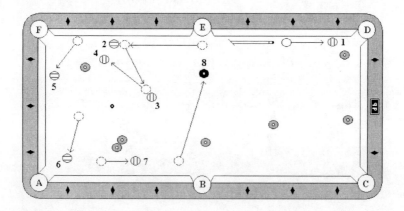

Figure 3-5 *Sequence*

One possible sequence for the run out is to play the first ball, marked 1, in corner pocket D. Use draw english to get shape on the second ball. Play the second ball in corner pocket F, using stop english. Play the third ball in side pocket B, also using stop. The fourth ball is played in corner pocket F, using moderate follow english to get shape on the fifth ball. Play the fifth ball in corner pocket A. Here slight follow english will bring the cue ball off the rail for shape on the sixth ball. Play the sixth ball in corner pocket A, using low left. The seventh ball is played in corner pocket C, using follow. And, for the win, make the 8 ball in side pocket E, using either follow or stop. Easy stuff.

Strategy Four

Although Eight Ball can be full of challenging shots and positions, the ideal run consists of short and medium shots with mostly follow and stop english, like those depicted in Figure 3-5. Long shots, combination shots, kiss shots—all three ball shots—are your enemy, as are massé and jump shots. Avoid them.

6. CLUSTERS

Clusters are two or more balls in extremely close proximity to each other; some may even be touching (Figure 3-6).

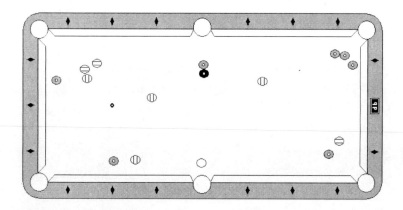

Figure 3-6 *Clusters*

Strategy One

If your opponent's group has a cluster, play around it, trying your best not to break it up. This may force your opponent to waste a shot, or at least, a position play. Don't do him or her any favors.

Strategy Two

If you are stuck with a group that has clusters, they must be broken up as early in the game as possible. If you run five balls then miss the sixth because it was in a two-ball cluster, you will leave your opponent with an unobstructed table on which to run out and win.

Winning Tip
If you are stuck with a group that has clusters, they must be broken up as early in the game as possible.

The patterns and clusters in Figure 3-6 are dreadful; there are a few iffy shots that may or may not go in. But, if you play the first ball into corner pocket C, and carom the cue ball to break up the three ball cluster by corner pocket D (Figure 3-7), you can plot your sequence from there and continue with a run out.

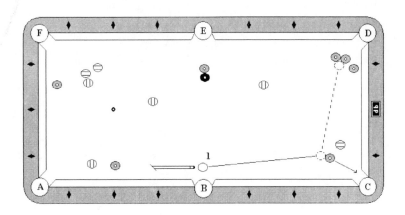

Figure 3-7 *Cluster break up*

Or, if the shot doesn't break up the cluster, you can play a defensive safe or safety for your second shot and let your opponent worry about the other cluster at pocket F.

Strategy Three

Eight Ball clusters consist of your balls, your opponent's balls, the 8 ball, or some combination of the three.

Examine the cluster closely. Look for dead combination shots or dead frozen balls. These are balls that will fall into a pocket when the cluster is hit, usually from any place on the table, which will allow you to break open the cluster and continue to shoot.

If a cluster contains only your balls, try to break it up early.

If a cluster contains only your opponent's balls, don't touch it without good reason, like you need the cluster to play safe, or to get shape for a run out, and so on. Usually, though, the strategy is to leave the cluster alone.

If a cluster contains the 8 ball, be careful, and don't break it up until you have to. There's no reason to help your opponent.

If a cluster contains some combination of balls, you normally must treat it as if it contains only your balls. Often, though, especially in Eight Ball, you can sneak the cue ball within the cluster and shoot your ball out leaving the remaining balls for your opponent to worry about, and look like a genius' offspring at the same time.

Whatever you do, don't try to blast into a cluster and hope for the best without analyzing it first. It'll create more problems than it'll solve. Maintain control, shoot softly, pay attention, and don't count on luck.

7. KEY BALL

Some players feel that the key ball is any ball that solves a problem, that the key ball will help you get shape or break up a cluster or hinder your opponent. Although these can be considered key balls for a specific shot, they won't necessarily set you up to win the game. The real key ball in Eight Ball is a must make ball that, once made, puts you directly into position to win the game, and the only ball that can do this is the last ball in your group, the ball just prior to shooting the 8 ball.

Strategy

When you make your key ball, you must get into position to make the 8 ball. If you can't position the cue ball so you can make the 8 ball on the next shot, don't make the key ball. Shoot a safe shot of some kind, and do your best to leave your opponent without a shot, or at least with a difficult shot.

Winning Tip

If you can't position the cue ball so you can make the 8 ball on the next shot, don't make the key ball.

If you make your key ball then miss the 8 ball, your opponent needs only to make a good safe play to prevent you from having a shot on the 8 ball. Under some rules, if you miss the 8 ball or fail to send it to a rail, you lose the game. It's a gift from you to your opponent. It should never happen as long as you're using your key ball to your advantage.

8. FOULS AND PENALTIES

INNING ENDING FOULS

Inning ending fouls are those that send you to your seat and allow your opponent a turn at the table. The very nature of penalties is punitive by giving the advantage to your opponent. But, in some cases, if viewed properly, the advantage can be swung back to you.

Winning Tip

If viewed properly, the advantage of a penalty can be swung back to you.

Strategy One

Failing to pocket a ball is an inning ending foul in which your opponent must shoot from where the balls lie, as long as you made a legal shot.

This is simply missing a shot, but you can exploit it by using it as a safety. Just make sure you leave your opponent without a shot.

Strategy Two

Scratch shots, double strokes, push shots, interfering with the balls in play, shooting while balls are still in motion, failure to hit the proper object ball including the 8 ball, making the object

ball in the wrong pocket, jumping the object ball
off the table, making the wrong object ball, are all
inning ending fouls that allow your opponent to
take the cue ball in-
hand. Since illegally
made balls and balls
jumped off the table are
not spotted, these fouls
can also be used as
safety shots as long as
one or more of your
opponent's balls are
tied up to the point he
or she cannot run out.

Winning Tip
*It's fun to watch your
opponent's face when
you shoot the wrong ball
and say, "Oops. What
was I thinking?"*

   This is often called
dirty pool, but so what? It's fun to watch your
opponent's face when you shoot the wrong ball and
say, "Oops. What was I thinking?" as you walk
away from the table. Especially when they have
ball-in-hand and still don't have a decent shot.

Strategy Three
   The most common rule still played in many
homes and bars stipulates that if you foul, your
opponent gets the cue ball in-hand and must place
it behind the head string (bulk area or kitchen),
instead of anywhere on the table, and that he or she
isn't allowed shoot any ball, including the 8 ball,
lying within this bulk area. Players who insist on

this rule mistakenly believe it favors the better player, but it actually favors the smarter player. In this case, if you can't complete your run to win, play a safe or a safety, your strategy is to deliberately foul when your opponent's next ball (especially if it's the 8 ball) is within the bulk area. This will force him or her to bank for the shot. If your opponent misses, you are in a better position to run out, or in the case of some rules, you win.

A more sensible version of this rule is, if the opponent's next ball is within the balk area, it's spotted. Your strategy in this case might be the same if you are sure your opponent has difficulty making spot shots, or if there are balls already spotted that will hinder the newly spotted ball. Otherwise, you must rely on legal safes, or safeties, and not fouls.

Strategy Four

Any attempt to jump or curve (massé or otherwise) the cue ball over or around any object ball that causes that object ball move, for any reason, is an inning ending foul.

Dumb. Dumb. Dumb. These are the worst kinds of three ball shots and, like all three ball shots, should be avoided, avoided, avoided in any game in which you are trying to win.

To foul trying one of these shots shows poorer judgment than trying the shot in the first place.

GAME LOSING FOULS

You guessed it: one foul and you lose. Be astutely aware of all fouls, but particularly game losing fouls.

Pocketing the 8 ball before all other balls of a chosen group, except on the break (usually), will lose the game for you. As will, making the 8 ball in any pocket other than the one called, causing the 8 ball to leave the table at anytime except on the break, or making the 8 ball on the same stroke as the last ball in your group. There could be others depending on where you play, make sure you know what they are before you start the game.

Winning Tip

The only excuse for losing a game is missing a tough shot.

The only excuse for losing a game is missing a tough shot. Winners don't give up games by making any of these avoidable game losing fouls. Think about it. It's like running out of fuel in an airplane. It only happens when you're not planning ahead, and you'll get your nose bloodied every time.

Strategy

However, (except for the running out of fuel part) there are always exceptions. Even some game ending fouls can be used to your advantage. In some houses, simply missing the 8 ball, failing to send it to a rail, or scratching while playing it are game losing fouls.

If your opponent is down to the 8 ball, and you can't make a run out to win, simply play a good safe or safety shot, leaving your opponent with no shot on the 8 ball. Dirty pool? You bet. This is the essence of dirty pool, because when your opponent misses, you win.

This sounds like simple advice, and it is. But I've seen countless players ignore this strategy and go for an impossible run out when all they have to do is play a good safe or safety to win. When they're my opponents, I just smile and say, "Nice try."

9. SAFETIES

In Eight Ball, there is a difference between a safety and playing safe.

A safety is a defensive shot in which a player sacrifices an opportunity to score in an attempt to leave his or her opponent with a miserable head pounding, hair pulling shot.

Winning Tip

A safety is a defensive shot that you must declare before you shoot. Playing safe is also a defensive shot, but it doesn't have to be called. In reality, it's a planned miss.

Safeties occur only when a player calls a safety before the shot. The player then legally strikes an object ball either sending it or the cue ball to a rail, or pocketing the called object ball. Any pocketed object ball stays down. The player gives up the right to shoot again by calling a safety, but the incoming player must shoot the balls as they lie.

If you don't declare the shot as a safety before you shoot, it isn't one; and, if you make the object ball, you continue to shoot.

Strategy One

You should be prepared to play a safety at any time during the game. In a situation like that shown in Figure 3-8 it would be extremely difficult to make your last ball and get shape to make the 8 ball.

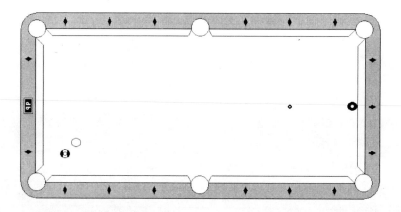

Figure 3-8 *Key ball shot*

You could try making the striped ball in the corner pocket by shooting hard to force the cue ball to rebound to the other end of the table, or your could try drawing the cue ball back to the other end (Figure 3-9). Both shots are possible on a seven- or even eight-foot table, though maybe not your best option. On a nine-foot table, however, they are both difficult and low percentage shots, where a miss will set your opponent up for a win.

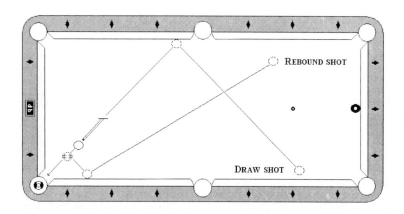

Figure 3-9 *Difficult position play*

Instead, this is an ideal time to play a safety. Simply declare it a safety and play your ball in the corner pocket (Figure 3-10).

Use low english and only shoot hard enough to make your ball, which will allow the cue ball to roll up to the head rail. Your opponent's only shot will be to try a long bank, and, depending on specific rules, will have to make contact with the 8 ball or lose.

This is only one example; safeties can, and should, be played anytime during the game when it will swing the advantage back to you.

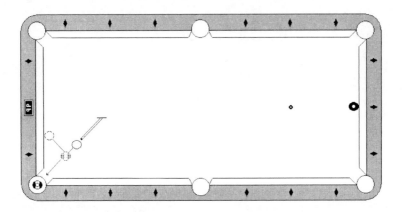

Figure 3-10 *Play a safety*

A safety is a tactical shot that allows you to play safe and make a ball at the same time. If you choose to make a safety shot, make sure you leave your opponent without a shot. Don't give up your turn and leave your opponent with an out.

Safeties are by design defensive shots, but there are still many, many players who consider them as *dirty pool*. How nice. You have to love playing players who always "play for the ball" and refuse to play safeties. In the long run, you win.

Strategy Two

Playing safe is also a defensive shot. In reality, it's a planned miss so doesn't have to be declared.

In this example, you could also play a safe by nudging the striped ball into the pocket opening

and stopping the cue ball on the rail. You give up
the inning, true. But you leave your opponent with
an almost impossible shot, and, again depending on
specific rules, will have to make contact with the 8
ball or lose, and if he or she rolls the 8 ball and
makes what would have been a miraculous safe
shot, you'll have a duck striped ball from which to
get shape on the 8 ball (Figure 3-11).

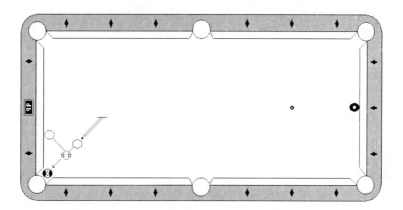

Figure 3-11 *Play safe*

If you want to play safe, simply shoot a legal
object ball, send it or the cue ball to a rail, and let
your opponent shoot. Since it doesn't matter one
way or the other whether or not you call a safety
when playing this shot, don't. Don't advertise your
intentions if you don't have to. There are two
reasons for this.

One, as stated above, some players still consider safeties, and certainly playing safe, as *dirty pool*, and could become ornery. Don't gloss over this thinking it's no longer true. Go out and play some of the "good ol' boys" in the dark and dreary bars in Small Town, Arizona, New Mexico, Texas, and Mexico. If they say safeties aren't legal, they're not.

Winning Tip

Since it doesn't matter whether or not you call a safety when playing a safe shot, don't.

Two, if you are good enough to play safe with aplomb, why advertise? Why give your opponent a reason to walk away? Call some plausible shot, make your safe play, and act like you missed your called shot. Your opponent will see it as a bad shot and tag you as a terrible player. How sweet. Once your opponents determine that you can't play for beans, they'll start coasting and their concentration, and therefore their game, will crash and burn. (Kind of like running out of fuel in an airplane.)

Strategy Three

Figure 3-12, shows a situation where a safety would be an excellent shot if you were playing the 8 ball. Here, your opponent missed the last shot with two balls left, but, sorry to say, has blocked your win with the 10 ball.

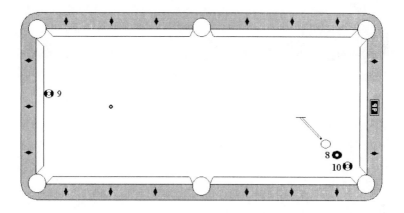

Figure 3-12 *Safety or not*

Simply declare a safety and make the 10 ball by shooting the 8 ball into it. Now your opponent must try a difficult long bank shot on the 9 ball. While it's not an easy shot, with a little luck it can be made.

However, understanding the rules could make your shot a sure winner, and eliminate any chance for your opposition to get lucky. Call the 8 ball in the corner pocket, play it into the 10 ball with straight on, follow english. The 8 ball will make the 10 ball, and the cue ball will hit the 8 ball a second time making it for the win. In most Eight Ball games, combinations involving the 8 ball are legal, as long as the 8 ball is hit first. Knowing the rules, all the rules, is essential when playing to win.

Even though I don't care for most three ball shots, these close-quarter combinations should be practiced and learned until they are second nature. A shot like this really shouldn't require much thought. Just walk up to it, bam, game over.

10. HANDICAPS

Playing to win versus taking handicaps may at first appear to be a contradiction in terms, but they aren't really. If your opponents don't at least feel like they have a sporting chance of winning, they won't hang around long.

Winning Tip

Calling all balls as a handicap isn't much to give up, because accidental or "slop" shots are truly rare.

Strategy One

One possible handicap to consider to make Eight Ball seem more accommodating to both players is that you (the more skillful player) must call all shots while the opponent calls only the 8 ball. If you think about it, although your opponents will believe you just gave them the world, this isn't much to give up. The reason: accidental or "slop" shots are truly rare. But when it does happen, don't tell them how lucky they were. Tell them how good their shots were. You want to make them believe that their luck shots were actually skillful, which will keep them feeling good about themselves, as their money becomes yours.

Strategy Two

Another possible handicap is the more skillful player must make the 1 ball or 15 ball (depending on which group you're shooting) in a designated side pocket, while the opponent plays his or hers in any pocket. This is a tough handicap; make sure you can win before giving up this much.

SUMMARY

In Eight Ball, shot selection is placed directly on your shoulders, because you choose which ball to shoot, and when.

Approach the table and ask yourself these questions. How can I win from here? Are the balls lying in such a way that I can run out? Will I have to make a ball or two then play safe? And, possibly the most important question of all: Since it doesn't matter how many balls are left on the table to win, *how can I force my opponent to lose*?

Winning Tip

Play aggressive when it's time to attack and play defense when it's time to safeguard.

Although it seems obvious that preventing your opponent from making the 8 ball might be as important as making it yourself, it's sometimes hard to convince yourself of it. But once you've found your best course of action, play aggressive when it's time to attack and play defense when it's time to safeguard. You're playing chess, not checkers. And you're *playing to win*.

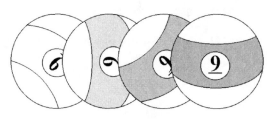

NINE BALL

Over the past twenty years or so, Nine Ball has become almost as popular as Eight Ball. It is an intensely fast game that can quickly improve your skills . . . and empty your wallet if you aren't careful, because it has become the money game of choice. Although the game's structured in such a way that allows any number of players, making it one of the few games that can be played by an odd number of people as well as an even number, it is rare to find a game with more than two players.

However, I have been in several "ring" games and they can be rather interesting. In El Cajon, California, Tom owned a medium size bar with two pool tables. He had a permanent nervous tick in his neck and as he got excited, it would pull to the left. When he played pool, he always appeared to be looking sideways, far to the left of the game, and was constantly dogging his shots. Tom always lost, and wealthy first and second year college students assumed he was an easy mark. To add to that assumption, Tom kept a stash of warped cues and would sneak one into a game now and again so he could dramatically break it when "the @#$%^&* pool gods are ignoring me!"

Every night, after losing a few games, to a newcomer, Tom would invite another "student from the university" into the game. Sure enough, Tom would continue dogging his shots, and always seemed to leave the second student with a winning shot or run out. Tom, his neck straining left, would break another cue and cuss like a madman, but he'd keep right on losing, along with the first student.

After the bar closed, Tom and the second student would meet for breakfast and split their take, which at times was considerable. Tom did all right for a guy who always lost.

So, if you find yourself in a ring game, look for the sucker. If you don't see one, you're it.

1. GAME OBJECTIVE

The game starts when the cue ball crosses the head string on the opening break, and ends when a player legally pockets the 9 ball. The 9 ball can be pocketed on the break or at any time throughout the game, as long as the lowest numbered ball still on the table is hit first.

Strategy

Prevailing wisdom stipulates that you should be an "all-around" player by running the rack from the 1 ball up to and including the 9 ball for the win, and that you should make a play for the 9 ball only if a can't-miss opportunity presents itself.

Winning Tip

A free ride is a shot where you can make your object ball and carom the cue ball into the 9 with a chance of making it.

Okay, that's true, to a point. If you're a professional or someone who can actually run nine balls, game after game after game. But most players are not professionals, and can rarely run nine balls, let alone game after game. So, why wait for a can't-miss opportunity to present itself? Of course it's not prudent to ride the 9 ball with every shot, but you should always be aware of where it is, and you should certainly look for position shots that will give you a free ride if there is any probability of making it, especially if a run out doesn't look viable. A free ride is a shot where you can make your object ball and carom the cue ball into the 9 ball with a chance of making it. Simply call both balls, make the object ball, and try for the 9. If the 9 ball falls, you win. If the 9 fails to go in, you can continue to shoot because you made your object ball. If you take a free ride, though, you must play position at the same time, or be prepared to play a safety on the next shot. Don't get lax and just whale away and hope the 9 ball goes in. Have a plan.

2. GAME PROCEDURE

Rack the first 9 balls (1 through 9) in a diamond shaped rack. The 1 ball is placed on the front apex of the diamond, and the 9 ball in the center. All other balls can be racked randomly (Figure 3-13).

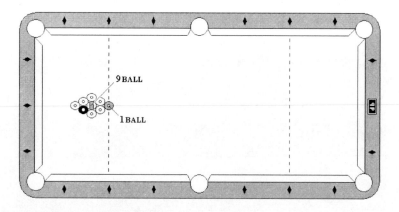

Figure 3-13 *Nine Ball rack*

Strategy One
Some rules call for the balls to be racked in some sequential order, like, 1, 2, 3, 4, 9, 5, 6, 7, 8, or some such variation. Because it groups the balls in the order in which they will be played, this arrangement gives an even greater advantage to the breaking player, as if a breaking player needs another advantage. Simply use the side break (explained below) to keep the cue ball in the center of the table. If a ball drops in, you could be in for

an easy run out. It's a gamble, though, because if nothing falls, you've left your opponent with a potential winner.

Strategy Two

Paying attention gives you a world of information about nuances or subtleties of the game. Take something as simple as where particular balls are racked as an example. The 1 ball must be racked at the apex and the 9 ball must be racked in the middle of the rack, and the remaining balls are to be racked randomly.

The 1 ball rarely falls on the break, but usually ends up in front of the rack, along with the cue ball. This is important to know for two reasons. One if no balls fall during your break, your opponent will have a shot at the 1 ball and, two, if any ball falls, you'll have a shot on the 1 ball. But, what happens if the 1 ball does fall? Where in the world is the 2 ball. Oh yeah! That little bugger would be next.

If it was racked in either spot directly behind the 9 ball, it will usually die and be left clustered with other balls or miserably buried behind what's left of the rack.

If, however, it was racked directly behind the 1 ball or at the tail of the rack, it has a good chance of breaking away from the rack and being somewhere around the cue ball, or at least at the same end of the table.

So, if you're racking for yourself try to position the 2 ball at the tail or behind the 1 ball. And, if you're racking for your opponent, where do you want it? You betcha, right behind the 9 ball. But, lordy, don't tell them what you're doing.

3. THE BREAK

As the game is played today, the winner breaks. Keep winning; keep breaking. This allows long runs from top players.

The breaking player has the cue ball behind the head string and *must* hit the 1 ball first. A legal break occurs if any ball is pocketed or at least four object balls strike a cushion. If the 9 ball is pocketed, the breaking player wins.

Strategy One

Usually, you want to make as many balls as possible on the break, including (hopefully) the 9 ball, without scratching. With a normal random rack, break hard and head-on into the 1 ball using slightly high english to force the cue ball through the rack (Figure 3-14). This breaks the rack effectively and yields an excellent chance at making the 9 ball on the break.

Winning Tip

You want to make as many balls as possible on the break, including the 9 ball, without scratching.

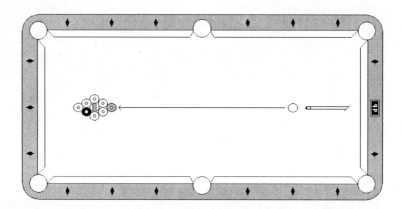

Figure 3-14 *Nine Ball head-on break*

Strategy Two

Breaking by hitting the 1 ball from one side of the table (Figure 3-15) and taking off a little steam not only seems to scatter the balls effectively but it also helps to control scratching. Although it gives you a slightly less chance of making the 9 ball, because the cue ball glances away from the rack, it improves your likelihood of getting shape on the 1 ball. This is particularly important if the balls are racked sequentially, because chances are that the 2 and 3 balls will be in close proximity to the 1 ball, and hopefully, the cue ball.

Place the cue ball four to six inches off either side rail, aim for a solid hit directly into the face of the 1 ball. Using low english to keep to cue ball in

the middle of the table gives you the best
possibility of making a ball or two, or three.

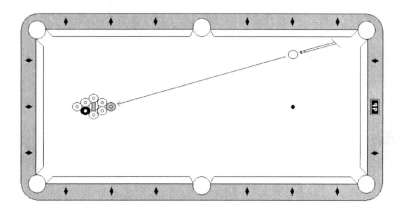

Figure 3-15 *Nine Ball side break*

Strategy Three

If the 1 ball is not struck first, all balls made
(except the 9 ball, which is spotted) stay down.
Current rules are that the incoming player has ball-
in-hand.

However, some rules still insist that the
incoming player gets the cue ball behind the head
string (balk area or kitchen), or can require the
breaking player to take the shot from behind the
head string. If your opponent breaks and you get
this option, make sure you have a good shot on the
9 ball, can run the balls to a win, or can play a good
safety. If you can't do any of these, let your

opponent take the shot, he or she probably can't either.

Strategy Four

The winner breaks rule is slowly starting to change to alternating break or loser breaks (and in some cases, the player trailing in total games breaks). Loser breaks unquestionably makes for a fairer game and is no doubt good for the spectator and television viewers, but can it be exploited to help you win? Absolutely. Most players can't run nine balls. (This is an empirical truism. If you want to prove it to yourself, go to any poolroom in the world and watch some games.) Let your opponent break and make three or four balls before missing. Now you only have to run five or six. Can you do that? You bet you can.

Winning Tip

Most players can't run nine balls, so let your opponent break and run three or four balls, then you only have to run five or six for the win.

4. AFTER THE BREAK

If you break the balls by hitting the 1 ball first and sending at least four object balls to a rail, but don't make any balls, *your opponent* can either shoot from where the balls lie or take a push out shot.

If you make a ball, *you* can either shoot from where the balls lie or take a push out shot.

The push out shot allows a player, immediately after the break and only after the break, to "push" the cue ball into position for a better shot at the proper object ball. However, after the push, the next player has the option of shooting or allowing the pushing player to continue to shoot.

Winning Tip

The push out shot allows a player, immediately after the break and only after the break, to "push" the cue ball into position for a better shot at the proper object ball.

Strategy One

If your opponent pushes out leaving you with the option to shoot, make sure you can run the balls to a win, make the 9 ball, or play a good safe shot. If you can't, let your opponent take the shot.

Safeties are usually the preferred shot over push out shots because you have more control over the cue ball, and it doesn't give your opponents any options; they must shoot from where you leave the balls. But if the push out shot becomes your best course of action, be aware that most rules are extremely vague on proper procedure. Some insist that you push the cue ball with the side of the cue tip. Don't pick it up and move it, and don't cue it in such a way that it might be construed as a shot. Simply roll the ball a few inches from its present position. Other rules allow you to cue the cue ball as if it were a shot, taking into account all fouls, except you don't have to hit the lowest ball or a rail. It doesn't matter which rule variation you use, just be clear before the game starts.

Winning Tip

When taking the push out option, try to leave a shot you can make but one your opponent will have trouble with.

A push out shot can be considered a safety in which you don't have to contact another ball or a rail. So, don't just walk up and touch the cue ball, or roll it an inch or two in some arbitrary direction.

Think about the next shot. Try to leave a shot you can make, but one your opponent will have trouble with.

Strategy Two

The push out rule is slowly changing to allow a push out shot to any incoming player. This means that after a missed shot, your opponent will have the push out option. At first glance, this appears to be an extremely harsh penalty for a foul. But maybe not, maybe it's really a winning player's dream. If you make a good safety, then your opponent pushes out, you can continue to shoot. You gotta love it.

Strategy Three

You must shoot all balls in sequential order. If you make a legal shot on the proper object ball, and your object ball is made, any other balls that fall stay down (excluding the uncalled 9 ball, which must be spotted) and you shoot again. The preferred rules have no requirement for calling shots as long as you strike the low ball first. However, the most common rules require all shots to be called, ball and pocket. Kisses, caroms, cushions, and combinations need not be stated if the ball and pocket are called, but bank shots must be declared. There is also an antiquated rule still being played that stresses that everything must be called including rail shots. This old rule may favor the more skillful player somewhat, but it tends to drag out the game more than it helps.

If your object ball is not pocketed, but you send any object ball or the cue ball to a rail, your opponent shoots the balls as they lie.

If, however, no balls contact a rail, or if you miss the object ball, a foul is committed and your opponent has ball-in-hand.

This penalty can be devastating. If your opponent has left you hooked to the point where you can't make even a safe shot and you miss everything, good for your opponent. Congratulate him or her and go on. However, you should never, ever, ever, put yourself into this kind of situation by dogging a shot, miscuing, or by simply missing an object ball. It shows a lack of concentration and a waning desire to win.

Winning Tip

Never hook yourself dogging a shot, miscuing, or by simply missing an object ball. It shows a lack of concentration and a waning desire to win.

Strategy Four

If you make the 9 ball illegally it is spotted (except on a coin-operated table where the next highest numbered ball becomes the winning ball), and your opponent has cue ball-in-hand. In some games, if the 9 ball is made accidentally while making a legal shot on your object ball, the 9 ball is spotted (except on a coin-operated table as above), but this time you continue to shoot.

However, you should never make the 9 ball "accidentally." Anytime you think your cue ball will come close to making the 9 ball, call it. Your opponent will look at you like you're nuts but if you make it, you can strut, and if you miss, there's usually no penalty. Of course the beauty of this is, if you make the object ball and not the 9 ball you continue to shoot. If,

Winning Tip
Never make a 9 ball "accidentally." Any time you think your cue ball will come close to making the 9 ball, call it.

however, you miss the object ball your opponent gets to shoot. So, don't overplay or underplay your shot just for a ride on the 9 ball, make sure you make the object ball.

5. PATTERNS

Repeating groups and sameness of the lay of the table become patterns (Figure 3-16), and you should be able to routinely recognize them.

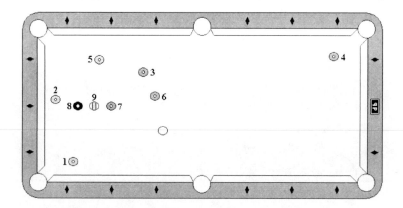

Figure 3-16 *Nine ball patterns*

You should also know, almost automatically, in what order within the pattern to shoot the balls to make them and to break up any clusters that may be a problem. In most games, this will determine your shot sequence. In Nine Ball, though, your sequence is always the same, lowest ball first. How you go about performing that sequence, however, is not predetermined and can win or lose you the game.

Strategy

After the break, carefully look at the lay of the table. Within it, you'll find straight-in shots, combination shots, bank shots, and carom shots. These same patterns will stand out somewhere on the table, no matter how many times the rack is broken.

Scanning the table and recognizing these patterns allows you to plan your sequence of shots, from a cue ball positioning standpoint, and should be your path of least resistance. If you play the 1 ball, you must get into position to play the 2 ball (or other lowest ball) next, and so forth, but you want to do this by using the simplest shot selection possible. Don't play banks, long shots, combination shots, etc., when they aren't needed.

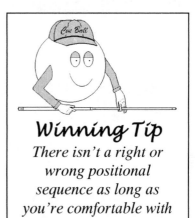

Winning Tip

There isn't a right or wrong positional sequence as long as you're comfortable with the one you have chosen.

However, there isn't a right or wrong positional sequence as long as you're comfortable with the one you have chosen, and if you are, you're on your way to winning. If you're uncomfortable with your selection, you're putting undue pressure on yourself, so play a safety and regroup.

A good sequence for Figure 3-16 is shown in Figure 3-17, all simple, straightforward, non-complicated shots.

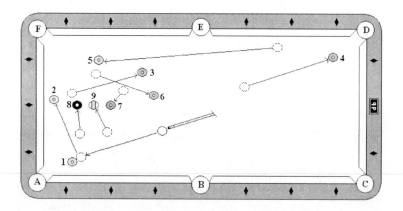

Figure 3-17 *Nine Ball positional sequence*

Play the 1 ball in corner pocket A, using stop english. Play the 2 ball in corner pocket F, using high right english. The 3 ball is played in side pocket E (or corner D depending on your shape), using follow english. Play the 4 ball in corner pocket D, using high left english. From there, play the 5 ball in corner pocket F, using stop; put the 6 ball in corner pocket C (or side pocket B, again depending on your shape), using draw; make the 7 ball in corner pocket A, using follow; play the 8 ball in corner F, using draw; and, for the win, shoot the 9 ball in corner pocket F (or in side pocket B, also depending on your shape), using stop.

Easy stuff.

6. CLUSTERS

Clusters are two or more balls in close proximity to each other; some may even be touching (Figure 3-18).

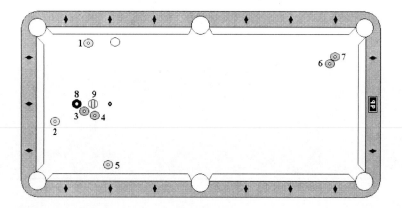

Figure 3-18 *Nine Ball cluster*

Strategy One
Unlike Eight Ball, where some clusters won't affect you at all, in Nine Ball, all clusters are potential headaches. So, if you don't think you can run out, don't break up any clusters, play a safe shot instead. This will force your opponent to not only play from your leave, but also to waste a shot or position play trying to break up the cluster. In

Figure 3-18, after only two or three shots, the 3, 4, 8, and 9 ball cluster will have to be dealt with.

Strategy Two

If, after the break, you're stuck with a cluster, in most cases it should be broken up as early in the game as possible. If you run five or six balls then miss the next one because it was in a cluster, you will leave your opponent with an unobstructed table on which to run out and win.

Often, though, it could be advantageous to leave the cluster until later, toward the end of your run maybe, if you have a perfect breakout ball there.

Notice the 6 and 7 ball cluster in Figure 3-18. A cluster like that, of course, doesn't have to be broken up, because the 7 ball can be made off the 6 from almost anywhere on the table. If they were reversed, though, you might have to consider some kind of break up, combination, or carom shot to make the 6 ball early. Just make sure you make your primary object ball first.

Strategy Three

Although, only nine shots are needed for a run out to win in Nine Ball, they can be difficult because the balls must be played in sequential order. So start with the money ball (9 ball unless you're playing with a handicap advantage) and plan your shots backward to determine your path of

Winning Tip

*Start with the money ball
and plan your shots
backward to determine
your path of least
resistance.*

least resistance. This will quickly tell you how many clusters must be dealt with and if you should play an early safe shot. Once a shot has been missed, or your opponent has taken a shot or two, you have to reassess because the lay of the table will change, as will clusters and patterns. But, again, the sequence always remains the same, low ball to high ball.

Strategy Four

In some cases, not all is lost because of clusters. In Figure 3-18 the 3, 4, 8, and 9 ball cluster looks forbidding. When and how do you break them apart? Try this (Figure 3-19): Play the 1 ball in corner pocket F, using slight high left english.

Play the 2 ball in corner pocket A, using stop or very slight high english. You don't want the cue ball to roll much past the spot vacated by the 2 ball. Now, using left or right draw english (depending on position), play the 3 ball into the 9 ball, making the 9 ball in side pocket E. Don't forget to call the 9 ball, and shoot only hard enough to make it. The 3 ball should stop where the 9 ball was and the cue ball should draw behind the 8 ball or 4 ball, depending on the english used. This will leave your opponent with a tough shot in case the 9 ball doesn't fall. What looked like a fiasco of clusters is really a perfect setup if you're paying attention.

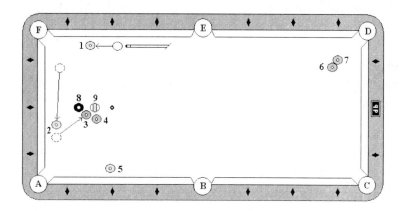

Figure 3-19 *A setup positional sequence*

7. KEY BALL

Usually, the ball before the 9 ball is your key ball. When you make the key ball, you must get

Winning Tip
In Nine Ball, your key ball is also your opponent's key ball.

position to make the 9 ball. If you cannot position the cue ball so you can make the 9 ball on the next shot, don't make the key ball. Shoot a good safe shot, and do your best to leave your opponent without a shot.

Remember, this ball is also your opponent's key ball.

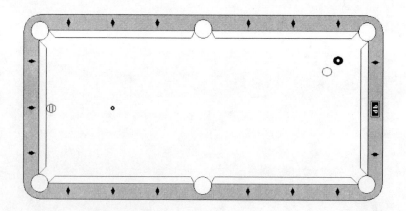

Figure 3-20 *Key ball shot*

In Figure 3-20, making the 8 ball and getting position to make the 9 ball can be done in a couple of ways. One is making the 8 ball in the corner pocket and drawing the cue ball back without scratching in the side pocket, then playing the 9 ball along the foot rail. Two is to cut the 8 ball in the corner, shooting hard so the cue ball will rebound to the

Winning Tip
Make your opponents beat you. Don't give them the games.

other end of the table to get some kind of weak position (Figure 3-21).

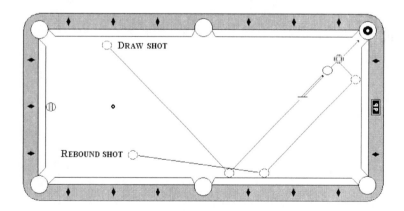

Figure 3-21 *Low percentage shots*

Both are difficult and dreadfully low percentage shots on a nine-foot table. On a seven- or eight-foot table, you might want to take the shot, but if you miss you lose.

Another way would be to lock the 8 ball against the rail, and leave the cue ball a few inches from it and parallel to the side rail (Figure 3-22). Use low english and shoot only hard enough to roll the 8 ball up to the head rail, and rebound the cue ball so there is no angle on the 8 ball. This way your opponent has to make some miraculous bank or kick shot to stay in the game.

In other words, make your opponents beat you, don't give them any games.

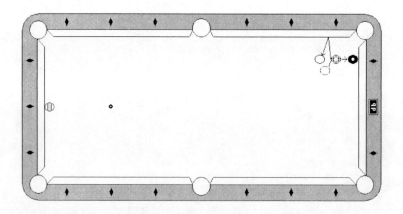

Figure 3-22 *Play safe*

8. FOULS AND PENALTIES

INNING ENDING FOULS

Inning ending fouls are more critical in Nine Ball than in most games because they could ultimately lose you the game. Any foul that gives your opponent ball-in-hand *anywhere* on the table is critical.

Failure to hit the proper object ball (lowest ball), failure to send any ball to a cushion after striking the proper object ball, scratches, double strokes, push shots, balls jumped from the table, interfering with

Winning Tip

Any foul that gives your opponent ball-in-hand anywhere on the table is critical.

the balls in play, and shooting while any ball is still in motion are all inning ending fouls. And as such, your opponent gets to place the cue ball anywhere on the table he or she chooses, except it cannot touch another object ball.

Strategy One

Generally, all but *failure to hit the proper object ball* are fouls that should never happen to you. These kinds of mistakes brought on by your own hand show a complete lack of concentration and lack of willingness to pay attention to the game long enough to win. When this starts to happen, it's time to go home.

A *failure to hit the proper object ball* foul is hard to take, but excusable if your opponent leaves you hopelessly hooked, with no shot at the object ball.

Strategy Two

In some situations, though, smart players can use these fouls to their advantage. In Figure 3-23, your opponent has made the 1 and 2 balls and missed the 3 ball trying to get shape on the 4, but left you with a horrible leave. No matter what you do, your opponent will get ball-in-hand.

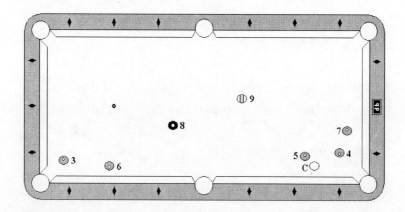

Figure 3-23 *Horrible leave*

You could try one of those massé shots you've been practicing on your brother-in-law's pool table. But, if you miss, you go down. It's like those idiotic jump shots you see pros using these days. They're pretty when they work, heck they're pretty even if they don't work, but in the long run, they'll cause more trouble than they'll save.

Now is the time to think *dirty pool.* Nudge the 4 ball close to the 7 ball, preferably between the rail and the 7 ball. It doesn't matter if you scratch, you've fouled anyway (Figure 3-24).

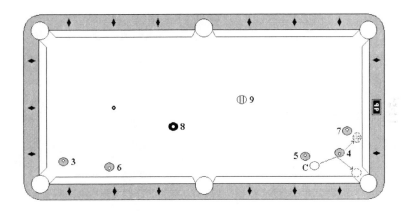

Figure 3-24 *Dirty Pool*

So what if your opponent gets ball-in-hand at this point. What is he or she going to do with it, make the 3 ball? Then what? The 4 ball is tied up.

What should have been your opponent's advantage isn't. This is dirty pool at its best.

Never accept a shot without examining it completely. Ask yourself how can it be turned into your advantage.

Strategy Three

When your opponents make an inning ending foul, count your blessings, don't laugh, and don't forget to tell them how unlucky they were as you pick up the cue ball to take advantage of the ball-in-hand penalty.

Winning Tip

When taking ball-in-hand, work on hard shots first.

When taking ball-in-hand, work on hard shots first. If you have a cluster that needs to be dealt with, set the cue ball inside the cluster and break it up from there, if possible; or set it where it can be caromed into the cluster; or break out a ball that's hindered in some other way.

If you pick the easy shots first, then miss the hard one, you're just giving the advantage back to your opponent.

GAME LOSING FOULS

Again, be astutely aware of all fouls, but be particularly aware of game losing ones. In Nine Ball, three consecutive inning ending fouls will lose you the game, so be mindful. After the second foul, you must make a legal shot, then you can make two more inning ending fouls, and so on.

Winning Tip

Be astutely aware of all fouls, but be particularly aware of game losing ones.

Strategy One

This rule stipulates that a warning must be given between the second and third fouls. If no warning is offered, the third foul is not a game loser, but simply another inning ending foul. If your opponent isn't paying attention, use this to your advantage.

Strategy Two

On the other hand, since you *are* paying attention to the game, your opponent will never foul three times in a row and not lose. Right?

9. SAFETIES

There isn't a specific safety shot in Nine Ball. There is the planned miss shot that most players refer to as a safety, but it doesn't have to be

Winning Tip

There isn't a specific safety shot in Nine Ball.

declared or stated to be legal. You must, however, send the cue ball or object ball to a rail after contact has been made. Then, the incoming player must shoot the balls where they lie. Of course, an unsuccessful safety attempt is a foul, and your opponent will get ball-in-hand.

Safe shots, like safeties, are defensive shots. The strategy is to leave the cue ball in a position where your opponent has a difficult shot, forcing him or her to foul or leave you with a good shot.

Also, since a safe shot doesn't have to be declared, don't. Why advertise your intentions? Keep your opponents guessing whether you played safe or simply missed the shot. If they think you missed, more power to you.

I've played in games where 8 ball safety rules were used, so they had to be declared. If these are the customary rules where you play, use them to your advantage.

10. HANDICAPS

As in any pool game, playing to win versus taking handicaps may at first appear to be a contradiction in terms, but they aren't really. If your opponent doesn't feel like he or she has at least a sporting chance of winning, you won't have an opponent or a game for long.

Strategy One
Like Eighty Ball, one possible handicap to consider making Nine Ball seem like a fairer game is that the more skillful player must call all shots while the opponent calls only the 9 ball. Also like Eight Ball, this sounds like an enormous handicap, but it really isn't much to give up if you are truly a skillful player because accidental or "slop" shots are rare. Most made shots are made in their intended pockets.

This is true in any pool game, but especially true in Nine Ball because you don't have the option of selecting which ball to shoot; you must shoot the lowest ball first.

Strategy Two
The most common handicap in Nine Ball is that the more skillful player gives the opponent an extra winning ball. That is, the opponent can win by pocketing either the 8 ball or the 9 ball. The greater

Winning Tip

*You want your opponent
to think he or she has at
least a sporting chance.*

the disparity of skill between the players, the more balls the skillful player can give up, say, the 7, 8, and 9 balls. Also, giving the opponent the 5 ball and the 9 ball favors the opponent slightly over giving up the 8 ball and the 9 ball. Use whatever combination will make the game seem fair to both players. Again, you want your opponent to think he or she has a chance.

Careful, though, don't giveaway the farm.

SUMMARY

In Nine Ball, game rules dictate your shot selection (sequence)—lowest ball first. But game rules don't dictate cue ball positioning. This is one of those things that separate winners from mere good players and good players from the masses of losers. Have a plan when you approach the table. Don't just shoot the next ball into the closest pocket without thinking about the following three or four shots. How do you get

Winning Tip

Plan your positional sequence every time you approach the table.

from one to the next, to the next, to the next? Plan your positional sequence every time you approach the table.

If you can't run out or make the 9 ball, where do you play safe? Maybe the first ball is the best place.

And, never play catch-up; always stay ahead of the game. One way to do that is to pay attention to your opponent. You can tell a great deal about your opponent by his or her selection and positional plays.

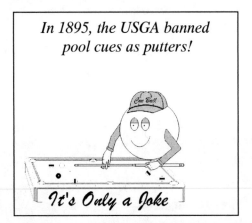

TEN WINNING
MENTAL FUNDAMENTALS

Some of the fundamentals covered in this chapter have been touched upon throughout this book. These ideas—motivation, knowledge, ability, confidence, attitude, pressure, concentration, body language, focus, and competition—although presented here individually for clarity, are closely related and should be thought of as a whole under the heading of . . . well, mental fundamentals.

These fundamentals are not only the psychological state you're in while playing the game, but, just as important, they're the mental state you project. Are you relaxed and confident of your shots? Are you uptight and unsure of your shot? One gives you a slight advantage; the other gives your opponents a slight advantage. Like a brick wall projects itself as solid, straight, and tough, you must project yourself as a winner. Take the advantage; don't give it away.

Of course, this works in reverse, too. Not only do you want to show a winning mental state, but you also want to consider your opponents' state of mind. Are they relaxed and sure of themselves? Are they up tight and unsure? Do they chalk their cues too much or too little? Just like in poker, these are tells. Usually they are subtle. Someone who talks too much, for instance, or too loudly, often do so because they are nervous. Little things can tell a lot. Keep your eyes open.

In a friendly game where everyone is just banging the balls around for the camaraderie, mental fundamentals are usually loosely observed, or even ignored. When this happens, your concentration, and therefore your shots, becomes sloppy. You revert to old, losing habits, which are then carried forward to your next game, where, suddenly, you can't make a decent shot. So, if you're *playing to win,* keep your mind in the game—every game.

Also, if you want to really dig deep into your psyche, read one of the many, many, many psych-yourself-up books available starting with the time-honored and excellent *Psycho-Cybernetics,* by Maxwell Maltz, and ending with one—or all—of the following more recent, and more to the point, volumes. *A Mind For Billiards,* one of Phil Capelle's outstanding pool books. *I Came to Win,* by "The Monk." Or, of course, anything written by Robert Byrne, just reading his descriptions of the games will psyche you up. But, in the meantime, if you simply want an empirical overview of how to mentally prepare yourself for any serious game you're about to encounter, then think about these following ten fundamentals.

1. MOTIVATION

Why play pool? Why do you play pool? What inspires you to play? It's certainly not for the exercise, I hope. So, how about love of the game?

Winning Tip

You can forget about friends and love of the game, because now only winning matters.

How about desire to win?

Sorry. You can't have both. It has to be one or the other. Which is it for you?

Sure, love of the game, friendship, camaraderie, and a social game now and again probably got you started. And if that's why you still play, meet me at Ron Moore's *Newstand Tavern* in Clarkdale, Arizona sometime and I'll show you why I still play. Oh, and bring money.

That leaves only desire to win. That's your motivation, your only motivation. If you want to play for any other reason, you'll enjoy the game, for sure, and the company, and the bragging rights to say, "I'm a really good pool player," but you won't win. Not consistently. Not when it counts.

I was playing a game in Bloomington, Indiana (just the other day, it seems) when the player who was slowly but surely sending me home without gas money was approached by a third player who said, "I'd give anything to be able to play as well as you do."

My competition looked the other player in the eye and said, "No you wouldn't. You're not motivated enough to give up all your spare time, all your evenings, all your weekends, all your friends, all your social life, and your marriage to practice the simple shots you're missing here, today. I'm sure you'd like to play as well as I do, but don't tell me you'd do anything to do it. I know better."

I'm sure his words were an exaggeration because I'm still married. To my first wife; the same sweet momma I married in nineteen . . . did I mention we have grandkids. Anyway, I've never forgotten his words, exaggerated or

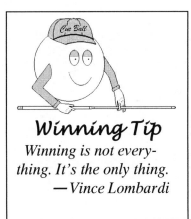

Winning Tip

Winning is not every-thing. It's the only thing.
— *Vince Lombardi*

not, it's something to think about. How much are you willing to give up to play to win?

If you play to win, you can forget about friends, camaraderie, social games, and you can forget about how much you love the game, too. Because now only winning matters. That's your motivation. It has to be, if winning is what you want to do. The great football coach, Vince Lombardi, once said, "Winning is not everything. It's the only thing." If you're not ready to think in those terms then you're not motivated enough to do what it takes to win consistently.

2. KNOWLEDGE

Knowledge of the game begins with comprehending the fundamentals, both physical (equipment, stance, bridge, etc.) and mental (motivation, confidence, ability, etc.), then progresses to thoroughly understanding the rules—not only what you think they are, but also what your opponent thinks they are—and how to use them to your advantage. This knowledge is then applied to practicing shots, cue ball positioning, determining patterns and sequences, and self-motivation.

Winning Tip

Knowledge is knowing the physical and mental fundamentals, and the rules and how to use them to your advantage.

Knowledge is gained by always being receptive to learning something new; a new way to make a shot, a different way to get shape, and so on. Watch some carom players. They think in terms of rails. They'll send a cue ball around the table to get shape. Did you ever see a Nine Ball player do that? Rarely, I'd say. Pay attention to snooker players. They can hook you with two balls on the table. These are only two examples. Look for a multitude of others in all games, and incorporate them into your game, and your thinking.

Knowledge is also knowing your limits. "A man's got to know his limitations," said Dirty Harry Callahan. It was only a movie, but it sure applies. During a game, don't try shots you aren't confident with. When you're playing to win, play shots that *will* win. I don't mean to say never take some risks if they are warranted, but don't play a risky shot if it isn't absolutely necessary, or if you have no chance of making it. Know what you can and can't do, before the game.

Knowledge then becomes understanding; understanding yourself, your ability, the game, and extends to understanding your competition and how they play.

3. ABILITY

Ability is your skill level, aptitude, or talent of the game. It's your physical and mental capability, whether natural or acquired, to perform with enough proficiency to win the game.

Some people are born with a certain amount of natural pool playing ability—above average eyesight, hand-eye coordination, grit, good looks (like me!), or whatever it is—but not any of those people

Winning Tip
You gain ability through practice and plying.

have the capacity to just step up to the table and win. That's an acquired ability, it's one that anyone can obtain, and it's done through practice.

Practice is probably the single most important thing you can do to build ability, confidence, and eliminate pressure. Your greatest performances will come from your love of day-to-day practice. Your practice sessions must be enjoyed as much as playing the game itself; they must produce their own rewards so they can inspire you to conquer shot after shot after shot. If you live for, or gain pleasure from, only the game itself; if you look at practice as drudgery, you'll never grow.

When it comes to pool, practice means to practice—repeated and systematic performance for the purpose of acquiring proficiency in shot making, cue ball positioning, and so on. Don't just mindlessly shoot at the balls and think you're practicing. Consider what you're doing, every shot, every stroke. Watch each ball to see where it goes, what it does, and understand why. If you're serious, be serious. If you're not, go home, or you'll become fodder for those who are serious.

And, don't spend too much time practicing what you're already good at. I've seen players who were good at draw shots play most of their shots with draw. They give up a little shape, or change their sequence slightly just to play a draw shot. They even practice these shots because it's easy for them, and it makes practice secessions easy. It's okay to be good at certain shots, just don't

Winning Tip

Practice your weakness, not what you're already good at.

sluff off an option of doing something better just for the sake of doing what you like, or what's easy, and that includes practicing. So, work on your weak shots, not your strong ones.

Also, running rack after rack is good practice, it helps with your aiming, positioning, and tempo, but practicing individual shots like rail shots, spot shots, throws, and so forth is extremely valuable. When you're running racks and a shot barely makes it, that's good enough, and you continue to shoot. But when you're practicing particular shots and a shot barely makes it, that's not good enough because here you're working for perfection, and you should accept nothing less. That's how you improve. Set up rail shots and shoot nothing but rails shots, a hundred of them, do the same for throws, banks, and so on. Thoroughly go through the practice shots laid out in Chapter 2. It won't take long until these shots are yours. Forever.

4. CONFIDENCE

Self-reliance, assurance, boldness, and self-esteem all show the confidence you have in yourself and your shot making, and your ability to play will show that you came to win.

Look at your impending shot as you approach a table, if you can make it, walk up to it, and make it. If you can't make the shot, look for another and play that one, or play safe. Don't ask for advice or stumble and stutter over possibilities and improbabilities during a game, leave that for practice. When you're playing a game, you either know the shots or you don't. If you don't, why demonstrate your weakness? You want to always show confidence, whether you have it or not. Don't let them see you sweat, right? Soon it will become habit.

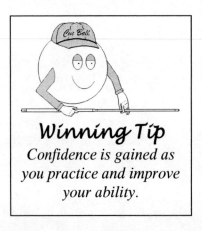

Winning Tip

Confidence is gained as you practice and improve your ability.

Although you must appear confident at all times, you can't just tell yourself to be confident and there you are: confident. It's something that you gain as you practice and improve your ability.

When you see a difficult shot, and know you have the ability to make it because you've done it a hundred times during practice, you'll exude confidence.

5. ATTITUDE

How you feel and talk about the game, the manner in which you play and conduct your actions, your disposition and emotion, whether negative or positive, will all show your attitude

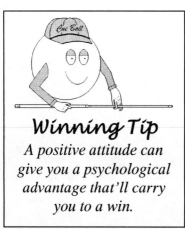

Winning Tip

A positive attitude can give you a psychological advantage that'll carry you to a win.

toward the game. If you have a positive attitude, you'll project confidence. If you have a negative attitude, you'll complain and berate the game, the equipment, and your abilities: "This table rolls off," "This cue sucks," "I can't shoot for shittim" (It's a wood). A positive attitude can give you a psychological advantage that'll carry you to a win, where a negative attitude could give your opponent the psychological advantage, dragging you down the path of the losing masses. I say masses with confidence because—here's an empirical observation—most people lose most of the time. If you don't believe that, go to any poolroom or bar, at anytime of the day, anywhere in the world, and observe.

Attitude shows by the way you play and interact with your opponent, friends, and the game itself.

Always be aware of your ability to play and win, and show it with poise, you don't have to strut like a barnyard rooster. It might intimidate some opponents, and even win you a match or two, but in the long run, it'll cost you games. If you want to be obnoxious, go play football.

Most of us have the same or near same physical skills that it takes to win a pool game or two. But it's attitude that holds the difference between ordinary players and great ones, between ones that lose consistently and ones that win consistently, between ones that control their mental and physical performance, and ones that don't.

6. PRESSURE

Most game pressure is undue and self-imposed. It is the burden of physical or mental distress you put on yourself to perform at some level, whether that level is obtainable or not.

Although a little pressure will make you perform at some higher plane than you would if there were no pressure (call it the magic of adrenaline), most self-imposed pressure cannot be overcome. Undue pressure brings anxiety, distress, or uneasiness, and then a fear of not performing up to your potential. It'll rob you of your concentration, your attitude, and ultimately, your ability.

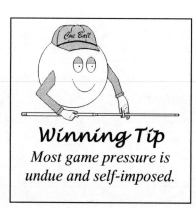

Winning Tip

Most game pressure is undue and self-imposed.

This usually happens because you're playing someone you know you can beat, and therefore, you *have* to beat. If your opponent is supposed to beat you, you'll be more relaxed and will perform well. This is the rationale used to explain why the opening games of a tournament can be tougher than the finals. Top players feel like they have to perform, they have to beat the underdogs; whereas, the underdogs feel less pressure because they're not necessarily supposed to win.

To deal with pressure, you have to distance yourself from the situation. If you walk up to a shot and can't quite see the right angle or aiming spot, walk away from the table. Go get a drink. Go to the bathroom. Do anything that'll take your mind off the game, the shot, or a must win situation. When you return, things will look much clearer, and a difficult shot will not only look easier it will be easier.

Also, unless you're an exhibitionist and get paid for your exhibition, never put yourself in a situation where you have to perform for anyone but yourself. This is one reason you should forget about three ball shots, jump shots, massé shots, and other trick shots that should be left to trick shot artists. If you make one, you'll be expected to make the next and the next and the next. If you can do it, that's great, but for most of us, it's pressure we don't need when we're playing to win.

Moreover, if you think you can beat someone, silently and with poise, prove it with your cue. If you start boasting that you could give Slow Moe the 5 ball and still take him to the cleaners, and now Slow Moe wants you to prove it . . . in front of a gallery, you've created unnecessary pressure for yourself. Winners don't need to boast.

7. CONCENTRATION

Concentration is singularly directing your attention toward the game at hand, and nothing else. You need to learn the mental and physical fundamentals so well that they become second nature, so you can concentrate solely on the game and opponent on hand.

Winning Tip

Forget the jokes and one-liners, and concentrate on the game, and on winning.

Again, if you are in a friendly game and you want to yuck it up and be cordial, that's fine. Just remember, it will affect later games. But if you want to win, forget the jokes and one-liners, and concentrate on the game, and on winning. Don't let friendly games steal your concentration, it takes time and perseverance to get it back. Playing friendly games to win, takes the fun out of the game, for sure. But you're not here for fun. Remember motivation?

Concentrating on your opponent and the whole game all the time is good advice, but that *does not* suggest that you should fixate on any one aspect of your game. If your cut shot isn't working, for example, do something else, don't fixate on it and let the rest of your game go to pot, too.

Winning Tip

Don't fixate on any one aspect of your game.

8. BODY LANGUAGE

Your body language is the tendency, orientation, posture, and movement of your body that expresses your desire to win (or lose) the game. In the beginning, body language is a mind-set that you develop by thinking about how you look. Do you look like a pool player?—a serious pool player? Do you look like you came to win? It's advertising. And if you're going to advertise, advertise a winner.

Winning Tip
Do you look like a pool player?—a serious pool player? Do you look like you came to win?

Did you ever see a movie where the actor picks up a pool cue and can't even make a decent bridge, or hold the cue properly, then proceeds to run the rack. You knew the minute he picked up the cue that he wasn't going to be the one to do all the amazing shooting that's required to run the rack, and that you could beat him out of whatever he got paid for his bad acting . . . in one game. That's body language. That's advertising, too. But not the kind you want. This actor is telling the world, "Look I can't really play this game, even though I think I'm good enough to fake it." Don't be a bad actor, unless you are acting!

Body language is also how you hold yourself, how you strut, and the rhythm you develop as you play. It's the rhythm of the strokes you take before each shot, it's the way you approach the table, and it's the way you move from shot to shot. Rhythm is the tone or tempo you set for yourself during the game, and whatever yours is—slow and methodical like Slow Moe, or fast and dynamic like Fast Eddie—don't let it be disrupted by your opponent or any onlookers. After hours, days, and months of practice, body language becomes an involuntary extension of your attitude, your confidence, and your ability.

Winning Tip

After hours, days, and months of practice, body language becomes an involuntary extension of your attitude, your confidence, and of course your ability.

And, of course, body language can advertise your opponents ability, stumbling over his or her cue reaching for another beer, dribbling on a shirt sleeve, but, "By golly, I'll play for twenty a game." And, since you've been drinking only water . . .

But, maybe you want to advertise that of a loser so you can "trap" your prey. Just remember this: You have to be a consistently solid winner before you can pretend to be a loser. It seems silly to me to act like a loser, and then lose! Learn to win first. Then if you want to take the chance of getting your face ripped off hustling, that's up to you.

9. FOCUS

Staying mentally in every game, every second of every minute of every hour is staying focused. You must pay attention to the table at all times, even when your opponent is shooting. If you don't, your mind will start to wander, and once you start thinking about tonight's dinner, you might as well hang up your cue and go have your steak,

Winning Tip

You must pay attention to the table at all times, even when your opponent is shooting.

because you're not focusing and you're not playing winning pool. If you let it, your mind will take you out of a game that you should win.

If you have to be reminded when it's your shot, or even if you approach the table and have no idea what your next shot is, you're not focused. Not only should you always have a shot in mind, but you should also be thinking of a sequence of shots. You should also know what your opponents were attempting, why they missed, what their sequence should have been, and, if you're really focused, you'll know why they missed before they even attempted their shots. When you're that focused, those opponents are yours for the taking.

Winning Tip
If you have to be reminded when it's your shot, you're not focused.

10. COMPETITION

"Know your competition." You've heard it a hundred times. In pool, though, because you don't always know who you'll be playing, it's not always possible. If, however, you are vigilant in you observation, it doesn't take long to get a feel for how your competition plays. Watching them approach their shots, hold and stroke their

Winning Tip

Staying focused on the game tells you what your competition is capable of, or not capable of, in shot order.

cues—their body language—will tell you a lot. Are they confident? Are they focused? Are they arrogant and overconfident? How much ability do they really have? Do they dog long shots? Do they play smart safes, or do they "go for the ball" on every shot?

Staying focused on the game tells you what your competition is capable of, or not capable of, in short order. And staying motivated enough to pay attention to your competition is gaining knowledge, ability, confidence, and a winning attitude.

SUMMARY

You cannot successfully have one mental fundamental without the others, and you cannot successfully have the whole without the parts. Each fundamental draws on the other, with all growing and expanding as you move from one to the next. As your knowledge increases so will your practice sessions, as your ability improves, so will your confidence, as your confidence expands, so will your attitude, and so on.

Winning Tip

I'd rather be good than lucky, any day. Then, when I make an excellent shot, I can smile and say, "I'd rather be lucky than good, any day."

Does this all sound trivial or intuitive? If you're a newbie, maybe not. But if you've been around awhile, it probably has a ring of "been there, done that" to it. Just remember, it never hurts to reevaluate, reconsider, and reestablish your game, especially your mental game.

I'd rather be good than lucky, any day. Then, when I make an excellent shot, I can smile and say, "I'd rather be lucky than good, any day."

And, here's something else to consider. Only after you thoroughly understand the fundamentals, only after they've become a permanent skill can you successfully modify them to suit yourself. If, for example—and I can't imagine why—you wanted to change your attitude to make it appear as if you didn't know what you were doing, you must first know the right way or you wouldn't know if your modified form was really wrong, or if it would even work. Learn the right way first, then you can become the great pretender.

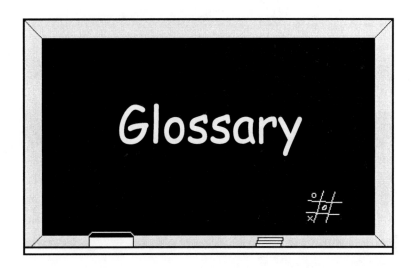

Angle of Approach

The angle at which a ball approaches its target, usually a rail, is the angle of approach.

Angle of Rebound

The angle at which a ball rebounds from its target, usually a rail, is the angle of rebound.

Balk Area (Kitchen)

The area between the head string and the head rail is the area of balk or "the kitchen." In most pool games, the first shot must originate from the balk area. In general pool games, it's also the area from which a player must shoot when he or she has the cue ball in-hand after the opponent has fouled. However, this is not true in Nine Ball, and in some rules, Eight Ball, where ball-in-hand means anywhere on the table.

The head string itself is not part of the balk area and, therefore, any ball lying on the head string is playable. The ball's lie is established by the center of the ball, not the circumference. This is significant for some variations of games like Eight Ball in which a ball cannot be played if it is in the balk area after a scratch.

Ball-In-Hand

Ball *in-hand* in most games means the cue ball is placed behind the head string in the balk area because the opponent has fouled.

In some games, such as Nine Ball and some variations of Eight Ball, *ball-in-hand* means the cue ball can be place anywhere on the table after the opponent has fouled.

A cue ball remains in-hand until the player shoots; that is, a player can move the cue ball as often as needed to facilitate the best possible shot.

Bank

A bank or bank shot is any shot that rebounds from a cushion. A bank is also where a smart player keeps his or her money.

BCA

Billiard Congress of America is America's most prominent pool and billiard regulating group.

Bed

The bed of a pool table is that part of the table that becomes the playing surface once the table is assembled.

Billiards

Billiards no longer refers to Carom games exclusively. Today, billiards encompasses all cue games including Carom, Pocket Billiards (pool), Snooker, etc.

Break Shot

The opening player takes the cue ball in-hand and makes the opening shot from anywhere in the balk area, or specific breaking area of certain games.

Called Shot

A shot declared by players before the shot is attempted.

When playing called shots, the shooter must call the ball and pocket in which he or she intends to make the ball. Calling the ball's path is not necessary; that is, calling kick shots, kiss shots, bank shots, or combination shots, etc. is not necessary as long as the object ball and pocket are declared.

Carom

Carom is the deflection of one ball from another ball, or from a cushion. Carom (originally called billiards) is a pool game in which the table has no pockets and the cue ball is caromed from object balls and cushions to score points.

Cloth Roll

A slow rolling ball follows the direction of the lie of the cloth's nap or weaving, at times making the table appear off level. This is often called nap roll.

Some cloth roll can be prevented by simply brushing the cloth in straight, even strokes from the head rail of the table to the foot rail.

Clusters

Clusters are two or more balls in extremely close proximity to each other; some may even be touching.

Common Fouls and Penalties

Except for a legal shot and cue ball in-hand repositioning, a player cannot contact any ball in play, and all balls on the playing surface are in play. This illegal contact includes touching with chalk, bridges, cues, hands, clothing, etc.

Push shots, and scratch shots, including jumping the cue ball are foul shots except where specific game rules state otherwise.

Double offenses during any given shot are penalized as only one foul. Also, any ball pocketed during a foul shot is not counted, and in some games must be spotted according to specific or general game rules.

Completion of Turn

A player's turn is not over until all balls, including the cue ball, are motionless.

Cone of Position

A position play in which you get close enough to the object ball to make it, even though the position may not be "perfect."

Cushion

The rubber attached to the inside of a rail and covered with cloth. The cushion is that part of the rail that rebounds the ball.

Cushion Nose

That part of the cushion that the balls contact is the cushion nose.

Diamond

A diamond is one of eighteen inlays (sights) on the top rail used to aid shot making. A Nine Ball rack is also called a diamond. My wife's wedding ring, on the other hand . . .

Dirty Pool

Dirty pool is a paradox (got a dictionary?). It hints at dishonest play, but in reality, there is no dishonesty or malice intended. It's simply a name given to that part of the game that's playing not to lose; it's taking whatever *legal* advantage you can conjure up for yourself to win. Dirty pool is part of the game, always has been, always will be.

Dirty pool is also that kidney shaped, green thing in my back yard!

Dogging a Shot

Missing a makable shot because you're not paying attention or you're trying position shots that are too difficult for the game.

Double Stroke

Hitting or stroking the cue ball twice with the same stroke is a double stroke, and is a foul.

Drag Shot

A drag shot is simply a draw shot.

English
   Spin imparted on the cue ball by cuing it off
center.

Facing
   The facings are flat laminated canvas, cork, or
such material that is attached to the end of the
cushions to deaden or prevent a ball from
rebounding from the pocket opening area of a pool
table.

Ferrule
   A sleeve or point installed on the end of a cue
shaft to prevent splitting or splintering.

Foot on the Floor
   A player is not to sit, lie, or entirely rest on the
table while shooting; one foot must be firmly on
the floor during the shot. Small or physically
disabled players who need steps, stools, chairs, etc.
to gain height may consider those devices as their
floor.

Foot Rail
   The end rail at the rack end of the table is the
foot rail. It is the end rail *without* the nameplate.

Free Ride

A free ride is a shot where you can make your object ball and carom the cue ball into the 9 ball, with a chance of making it. Call the 9 ball, if it goes in, you win. If the 9 ball misses, you continue to shoot; that is, as long as you make the object ball.

Head Rail

The head rail is the end rail at the break end of the table. It is the end rail that carries the nameplate.

House Rules

House rules are those set up by the establishment or owner of the table, and usually differ somewhat from the rules of tournament sanctioning or regulating bodies.

House rules occur for several reasons. Difference in equipment, obstacles around the table, and prevailing regional rules are three good examples. In other words, house rules reflect the rules favored by the house's particular situation.

Except in sanctioned tournaments in which rules are governed by the sanctioning bodies, house rules will prevail over all others, and should be agreed upon before the start of any game.

In-Hand

Ball *in-hand* refers to placing the cue ball behind the head string. *Ball-in-hand* refers to placing the cue ball anywhere on the table.

Joint

A joint is the connecting collars, pins, and screws of a two-piece cue, or simply where the butt and shaft are connected. A joint on a table is the seam of a multi-piece slate set.

A joint is also where I usually play pool.

Jumping the Cue Ball

Jumping the cue ball refers to causing the cue ball to leave the table and is considered a scratch and a foul.

Jump Shot

A jump shot is cuing the cue ball in such a way that it jumps an obstructing or blocking object ball. The cue ball must be cued from above to cause the jump; it cannot be lifted or lofted from beneath. The jump shot is legal in most games, but (hint, hint) not necessarily smart.

Key Ball

The key ball is any ball that changes the complexity and probably the outcome of the game. It is usually the ball before the winning ball.

Kitchen

Kitchen refers to the balk area, which is the area behind the head string. Also the galley of my yacht . . . if I owned one!

Lagging for Break

To decide the order of play, each player should lag by shooting a ball from behind the head string to the foot rail, rebounding it back toward the head rail. The player whose ball stops nearest the head cushion wins the lag, and may either accept or decline the break. Rebounding from more than one rail should not be a loss of the lag.

When more than two players are involved, players' rotation can also be determined by lag.

But it's easier to flip a coin.

Legal Shot

The cue ball must be struck first and with the cue tip to be a legal shot. It may be struck only once and cannot be impeded in any other manner. Imparting motion on the cue ball in any other way is considered a foul. Double strokes and push shots are fouls. All balls must be at rest before a legal shot can occur.

A legal shot occurs when a properly cued cue ball strikes a legal object ball sending either to a cushion, or pocketing the object ball.

Luck Shot

Any shot you take that you feel might or might not go in is a luck shot, because, simply put, it might or might not go in.

Massé Shot

A massé shot is extreme english put on a cue ball by elevating the cue butt 90° so the cue is perpendicular to the playing surface. A semi-massé shot is similar, but the cue butt is raised only 45°.

Massé shots should never be used in a serious game for two reasons. One, they are extreme low percentage or luck shots. Two, if by chance you are one of the few individuals who can actually make them, unless of course you're ready to go home, why would you want to do so in a game?

Miscue

A miscue is a stroke in which the cue tip slips from the cue ball. It is a dumb foul that should never happen.

Natural English

Natural english occurs when the cue ball is rolling or sliding (no side english) when it makes contact with the object ball.

Natural Positioning

Natural positioning is simply letting the cue ball roll to the next shot, without english.

Object Ball

The ball a player is shooting at.

Parallel Taper

Parallel taper is an oxymoron (what did you do with that dictionary?) used by some manufacturers to describe a pro taper.

Pool

Pool is the common name given to billiard games in general, and Pocket Billiards in particular.

Pro Taper

A pro taper is the narrow end of a cue shaft that has the same diameter as the tip, extending backwards eight to ten inches. A pro taper allows for a smooth and non-changing bridge grip on the cue.

Pull Shot

A pull shot is a massé shot that forces the cue ball backward without hitting an object ball.

Push Shot

Pushing the cue ball with the cue tip instead of cuing or stroking it is a push shot, and is a foul.

Push Out Shot

The push out shot allows a player, immediately after a Nine Ball break and only after the break, to "push" the cue ball into position for a better shot at the proper object ball, and the player must declare his or her intentions. However, after the push, the next player has the option of shooting or allowing the pushing player to continue to shoot from where the cue ball stopped.

When playing the push out shot, the cue ball cannot contact any other ball or rail.

Rack

A rack is the triangular or diamond shaped frame used to position the balls. The ball cluster itself after the triangle or diamond has been removed is also called a rack. Any device that holds the cues is a cue rack.

Rail Cloth

The billiard cloth attached to the rails is the rail cloth.

Regulation

Regulations are rules set by regulating bodies like the Billiard Congress of America (BCA). A regulation billiard or pool table, for example, is what the regulating body determines it to be for a given tournament; it is not necessarily a nine-foot table.

Running English

Running english refers to spin as it takes to a ball traveling around the table. Outside english will open a ball's rebound from each rail as it runs around the table.

Safe Shot

A safe shot is any legally missed shot used purposely by a player to hide or position the cue or object ball so the player's opponent will have a difficult shot, forcing the opponent to foul or leave the safe player with a good shot.

Safety

A safety is a defensive shot in which a player sacrifices an opportunity to score in an attempt to leave his or her opponent without a good shot.

Safeties occur only when a player calls a safety before the shot. Depending on the game, the player then legally strikes an object ball either sending it or the cue ball to a rail, or pocketing the called

object ball. Any pocketed object ball stays down.
The player gives up the right to shoot again by
calling a safety. The incoming player must shoot
the balls as they lie. An unsuccessful safety
attempt is considered a foul.

In some games, a player is allowed only two or
three consecutive safeties, then must make a legal
shot, playing "from safety," which must be
declared.

A safety should not be confused with a
defensive safe shot, as described above.

Scratch

A scratch shot is a foul shot in which the cue
ball leaves the playing surface.

Skid

When the cue tip strikes the cue ball, it will
transfer some of the chalk to the cue ball. If by
chance, that portion of the cue ball strikes the
object ball the chalk residue causes friction at the
contact point, forcing more english to take. The
object ball then "skids" from its intended path. The
remedy is to use only enough chalk for each shot,
and clean your (pool) balls regularly.

Slip-on Tips

Slip-on tips consist of thin-shelled ferrules and tips that slip over the original ferrules, or bare shaft ends of cues. And, yes, they play as bad as they look.

Snooker

Snooker is a pool game played on a large (usually 5 x 10 feet) table with six pockets, fifteen red balls and six numbered balls.

Snookered

A term used in Snooker meaning to hook or leave an opponent's ball hidden, insuring that the opponent is without a shot.

Spotted Balls

Illegally pocketed balls are spotted, first on the foot spot, then each frozen behind the other along the long string toward the foot rail. In some games, if more than one ball is spotted at a time they should be placed in numerical order with the lowest numbered ball toward the center of the table. In most games, however, numerical order is not a factor.

If the foot spot is occupied so that the spotted ball will touch any other ball, the spotted ball is to be placed as close as possible behind it, but still along the long string. Spotted balls should never displace balls in play.

Stun Shot

A stun shot occurs when the cue ball hits an object ball while the cue ball is still sliding, before english takes.

Three Ball Shot

A combination, kiss, jump, or any other shot involving more than the cue ball and one object ball. Avoid three ball shots if possible.

Most three ball shots are sucker shots and should be avoided.

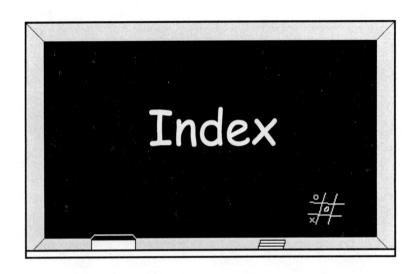

Index

ABOUT THE AUTHOR

 After three years in the U.S. Army's 101st Airborne division (1962-1965) jumping out of perfectly good airplanes and working on Huey helicopters, I married, had two daughters then attended Indiana University's School of Business in Bloomington, Indiana.

After Indiana University, I opened a twenty-four table billiard room in Indiana where I played on, sold, and serviced a variety of new, used, and antique tables.

In 1982, with one daughter in college and the other in high school, we moved to Arizona where I have remained in the billiard table service and repair business, and continued to play.

My wife and I have two granddaughters and two grandsons. Wow.

GIVE A GIFT THAT WILL BE
APPRECIATED FOR YEARS

CHECK WITH YOUR FAVORITE
BOOKSTORE, ONLINE BOOKSELLER
BILLIARD SUPPLIER, OR ORDER HERE

YES, please send me
___ *Dirty Pool: Playing to Win* at $24.95 each
___ *Buying or Selling a Pool Table* at $24.95 each
___ *The Billiard Guidebook* at $59.95 each
Shipping is **FREE**.
AND, we pay city and state sales tax.
Canadian orders must be in U.S. funds or postal
money order, plus $3.00 for shipping.
Allow 30 days for delivery.

My check or money order for $_____
is enclosed. Or charge my:
      ☐MasterCard, ☐Visa, ☐Discover
Card #_____
Exp. Date_____
Signature_____

Name_____
Organization_____
Address_____
City/State/Zip_____
Phone_____
Email_____

MAIL ORDERS
Copy this form, make checks payable and return
to:
Phoenix Billiards
6133 W. Port Au Prince Lane
Glendale, AZ 85306

ON LINE
WWW.PHOENIXBILLIARDS.COM

PHONE OR FAX CREDIT CARD ORDERS
Call: 1-800-449-0804
1-602-843-0804
Fax: 1-602-843-2625

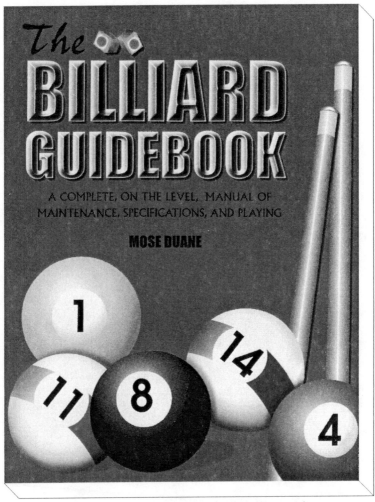

Size: 8½ X 11, 396 pages, 269 illustrations

The Billiard Guidebook thoroughly covers the structure of pool tables and equipment, and the complexities of table maintenance, specifications, moving, game fundamentals, and rules.

This definitive book on billiards is only $59.95.

Size 5½ X 8½, 178 pages, 61 illustrations

Buying or Selling a Pool Table is the most in-depth book on how to buy or sell a new or used table. There are several components (differences is playing surfaces, cushions, accessories, etc.) that must be looked at before a purchase or sale should be completed, and many buyers and sellers have no idea what those differences are.

This book is packed with solid information for only $24.95.